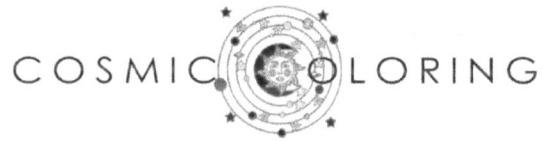

COSMIC COLORING

Adult Coloring Book

STRESS RELIEVING MAGICAL MANDALAS

Tap into your subconscious, and unleash your creative expression. Channel stress and anxiety into artistic creations. Escape to a world of inspiration, and endless possibilities.

Our dazzling designs will captivate both, beginners and advanced colorists. There are no instructions, no right, or wrong way. Color in any way you wish to create unique and exquisite pieces. Flip the switch off and lose yourself in the flow of coloring. Unwind and take your time, bring the color and let your imagination run free! These amazing, intricate designs are ready for you to add your own special touch. Find your bliss and create your masterpiece.

Features:

- No experience required. Just add color!

- 30 beautiful patterns, designed to spark your imagination and creativity.

- Pick a picture and start your journey to inner peace and relaxation.

- Printed on 8x10 paper. You'll have plenty of space for details.

- Printed with the reverse side blank. When you're finished, you will have a unique piece of art.

- Perfect for colored pencils, gel pens, markers, porous point pens or crayons.

- Share your passion!

For updates and release information, please visit us at

www.cosmiccoloringbooks.com
www.facebook.com/cosmiccoloringbooks

Happy Coloring!

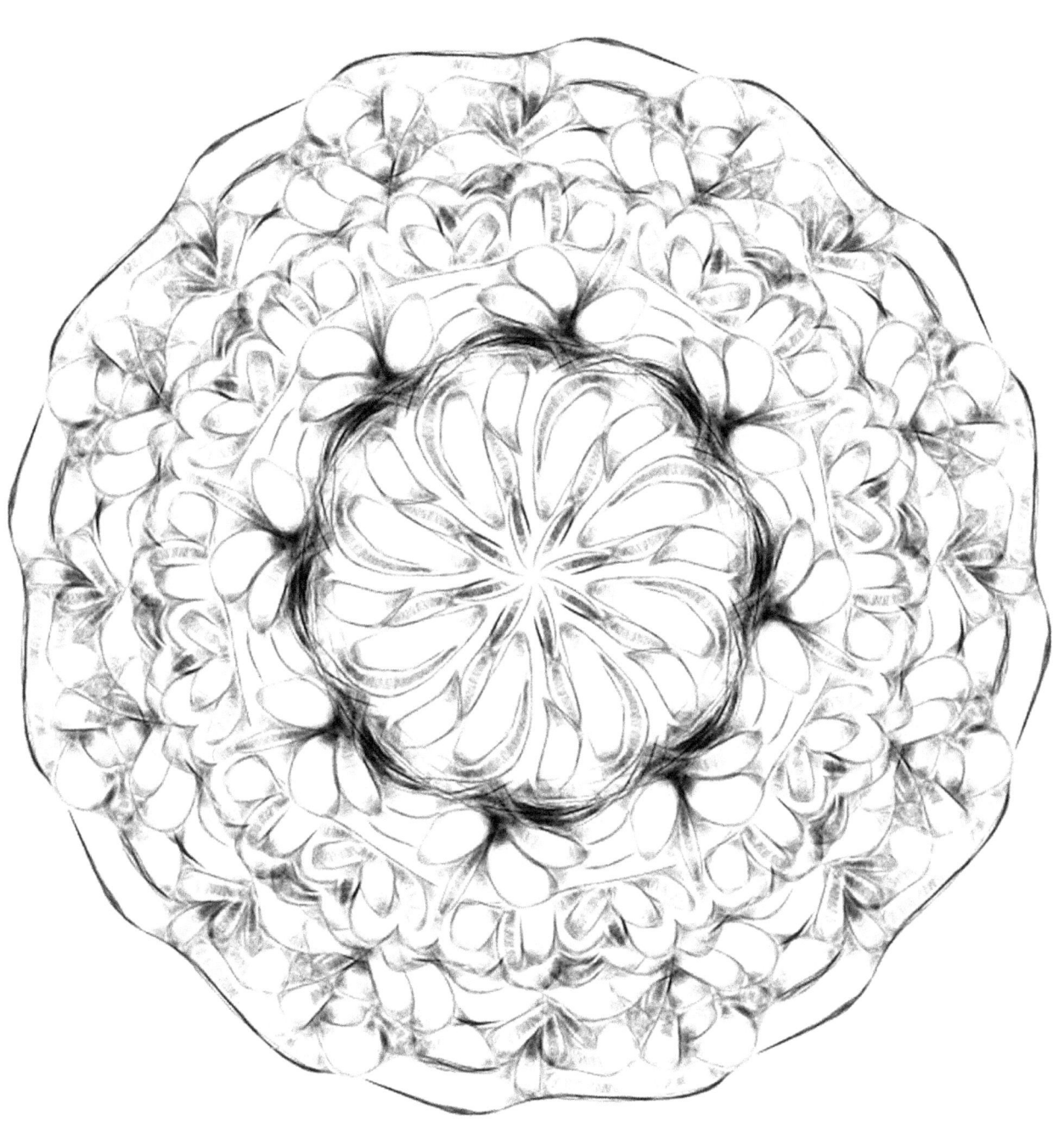

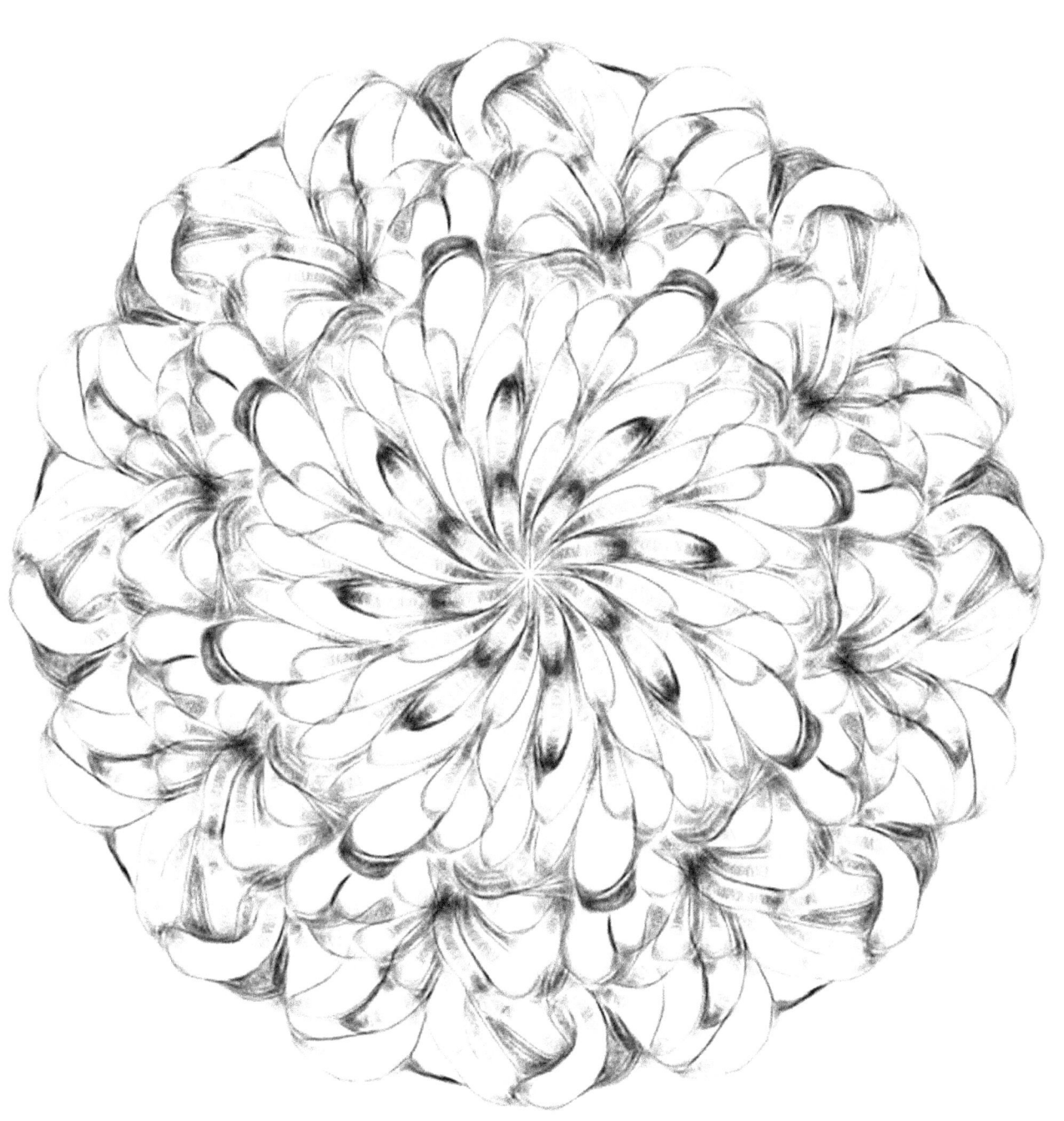

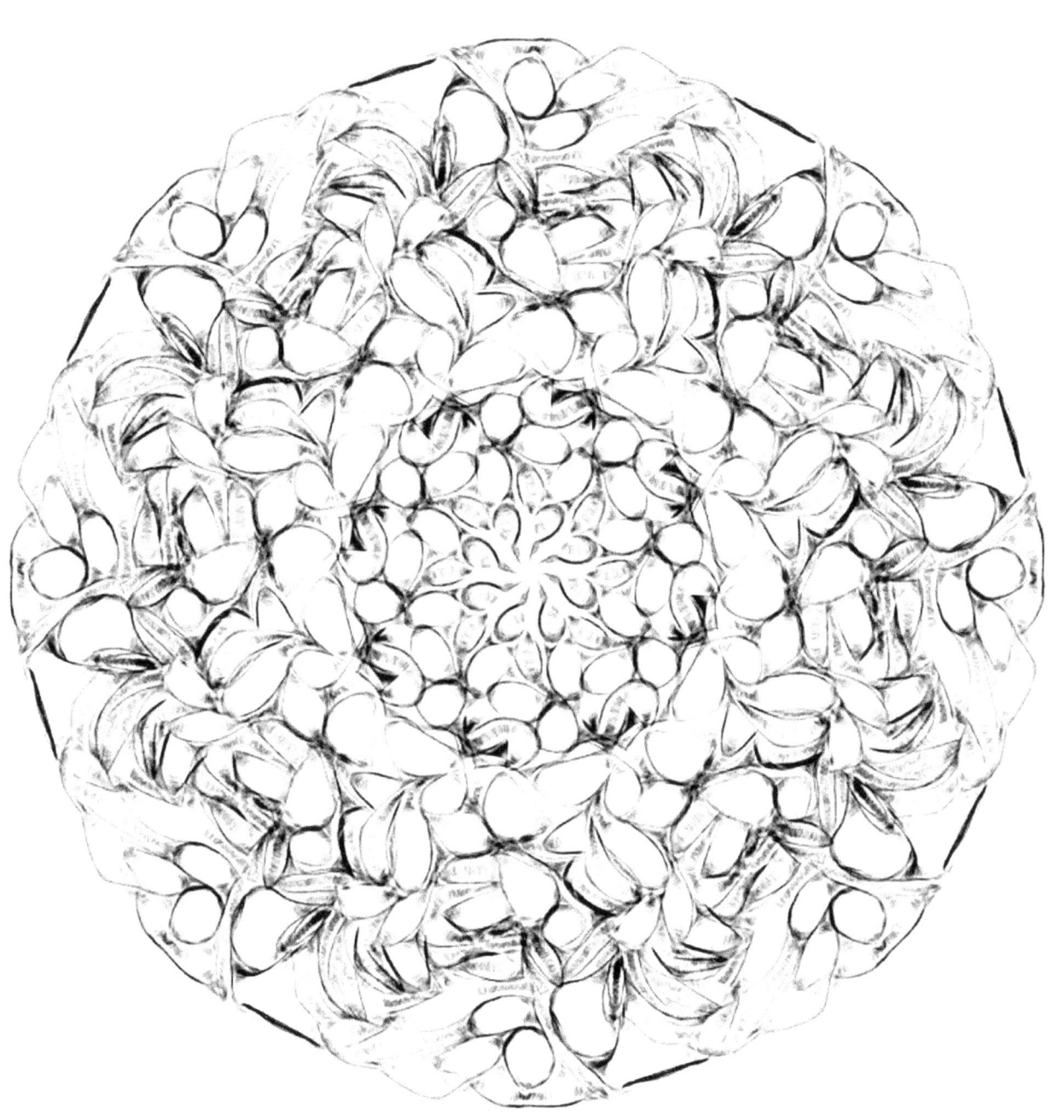

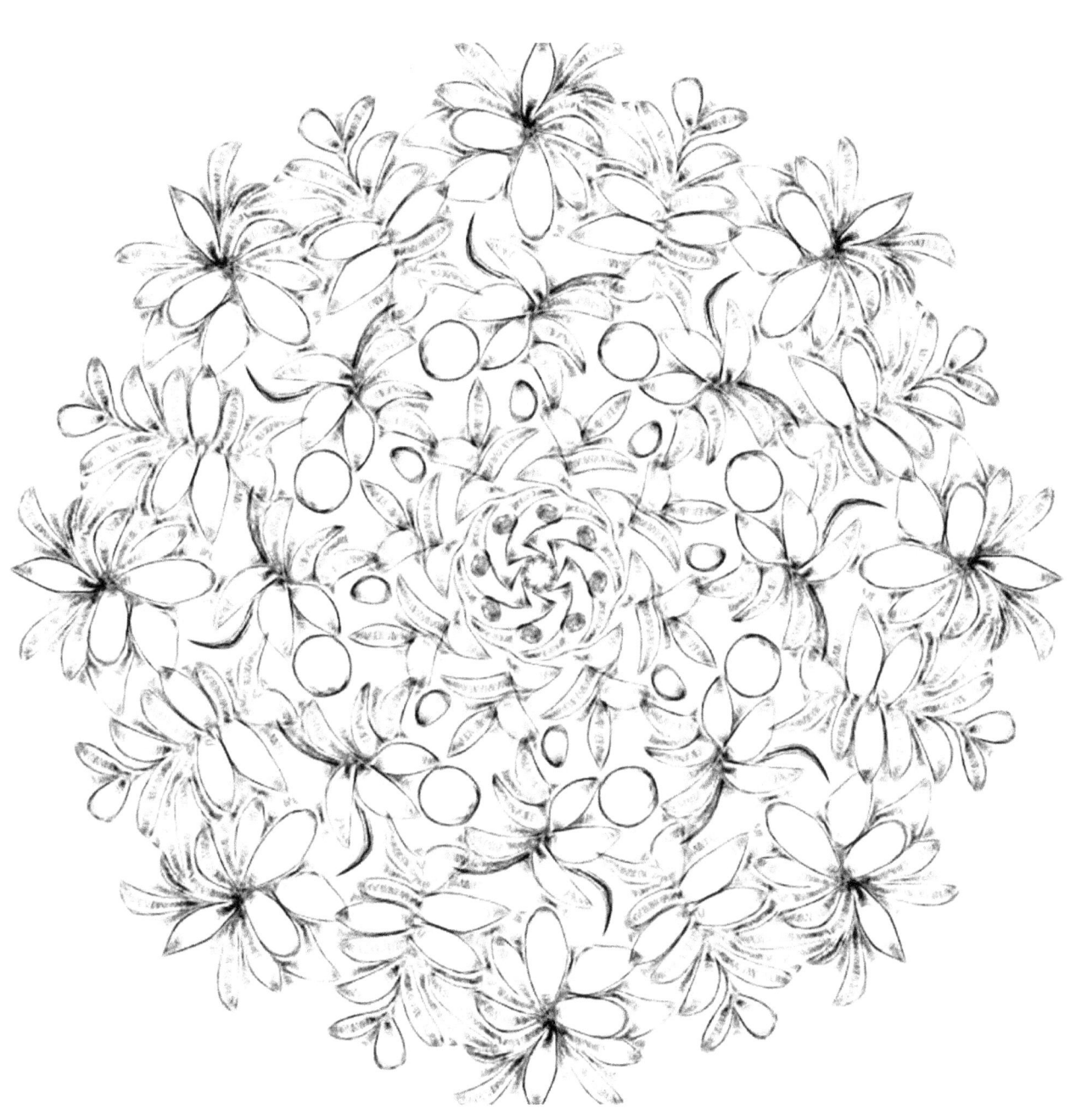

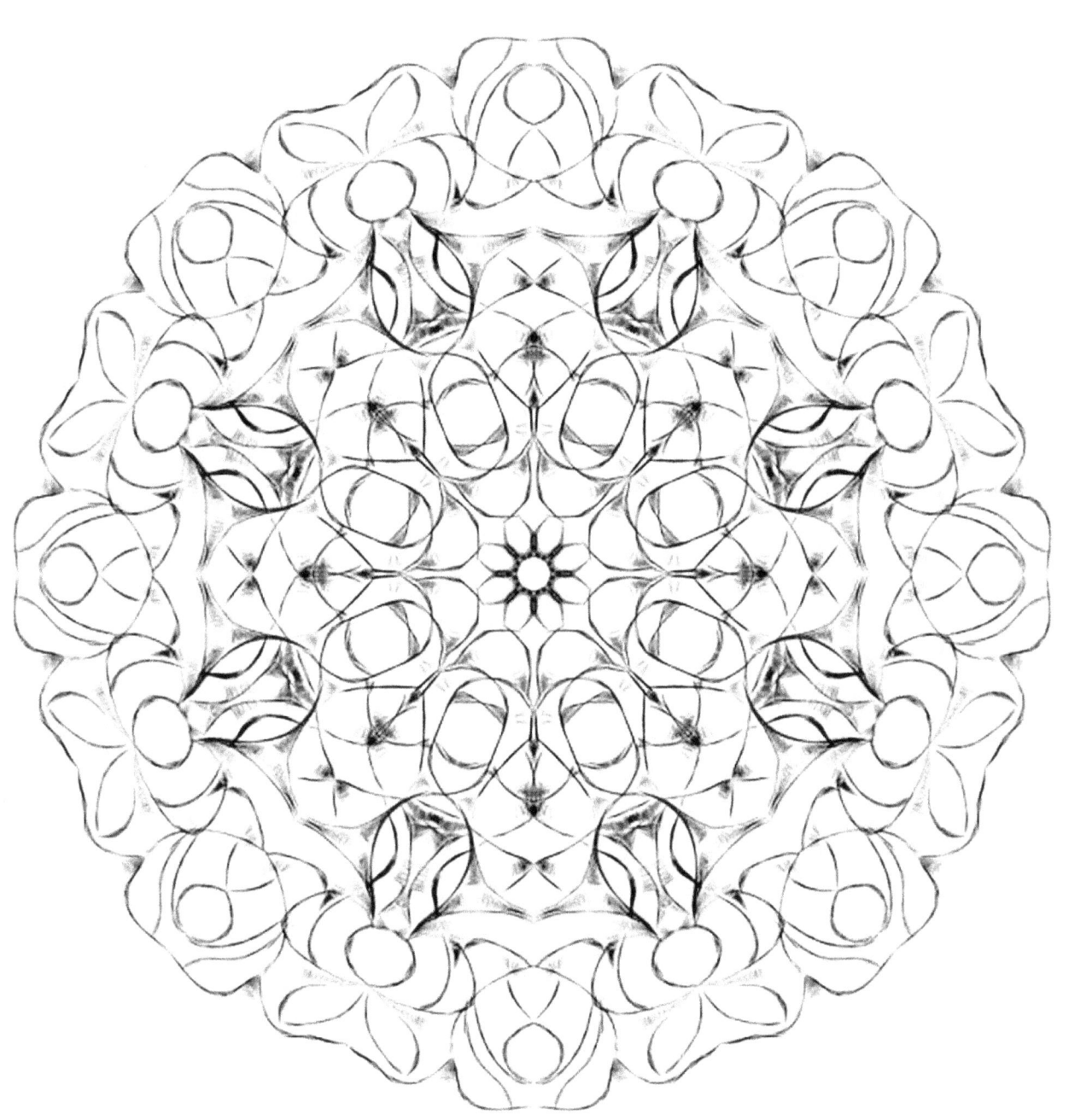

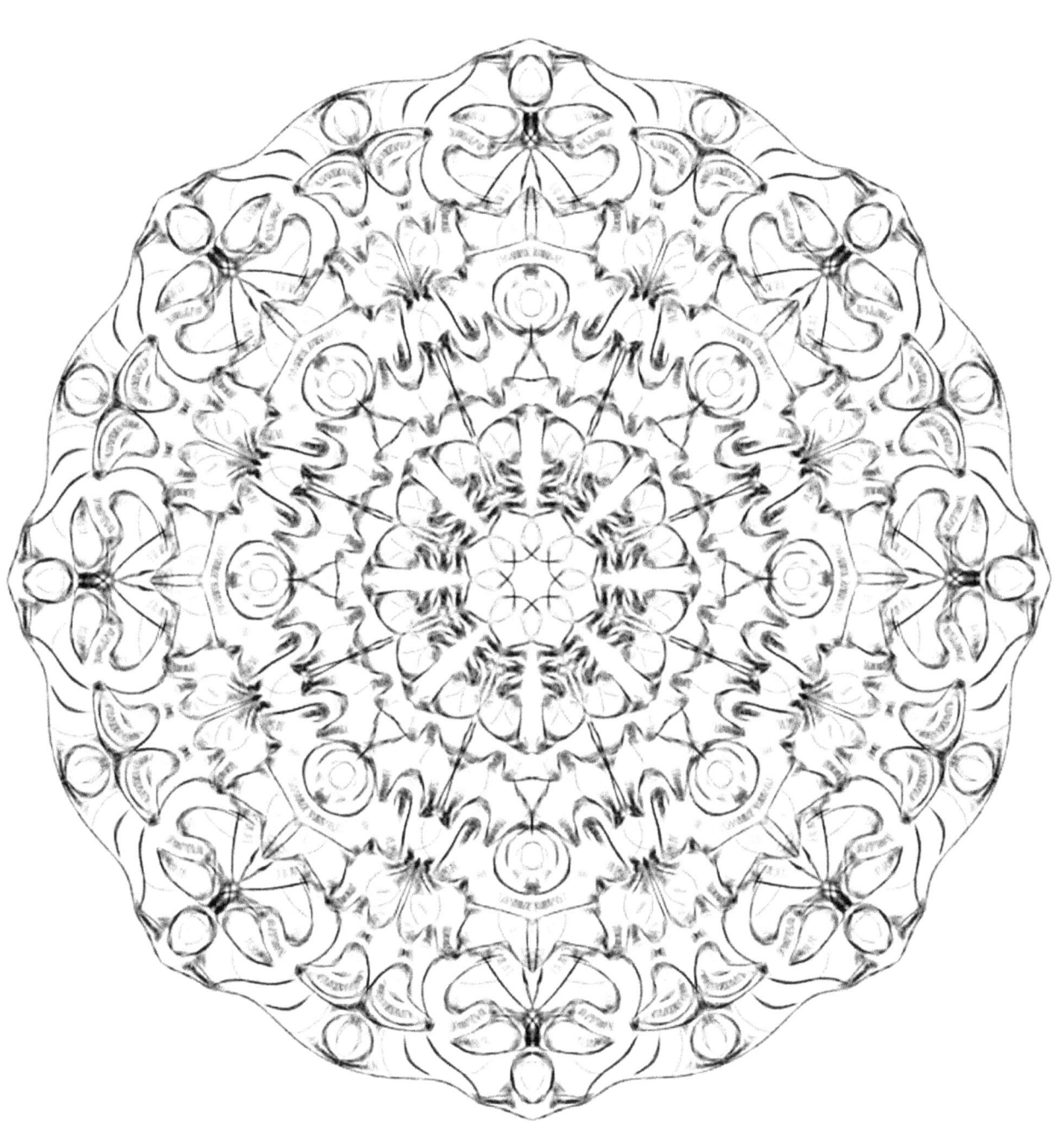

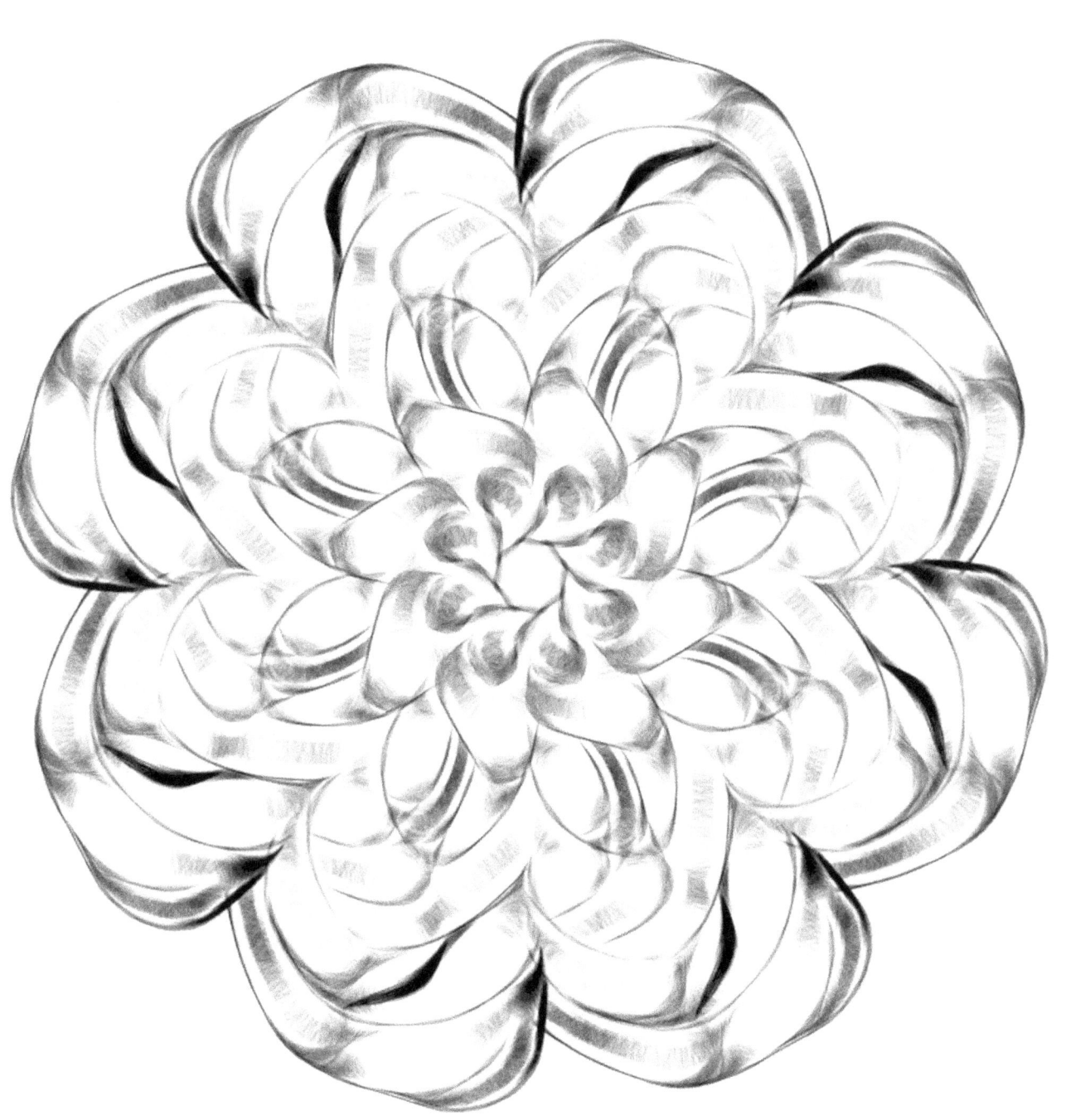

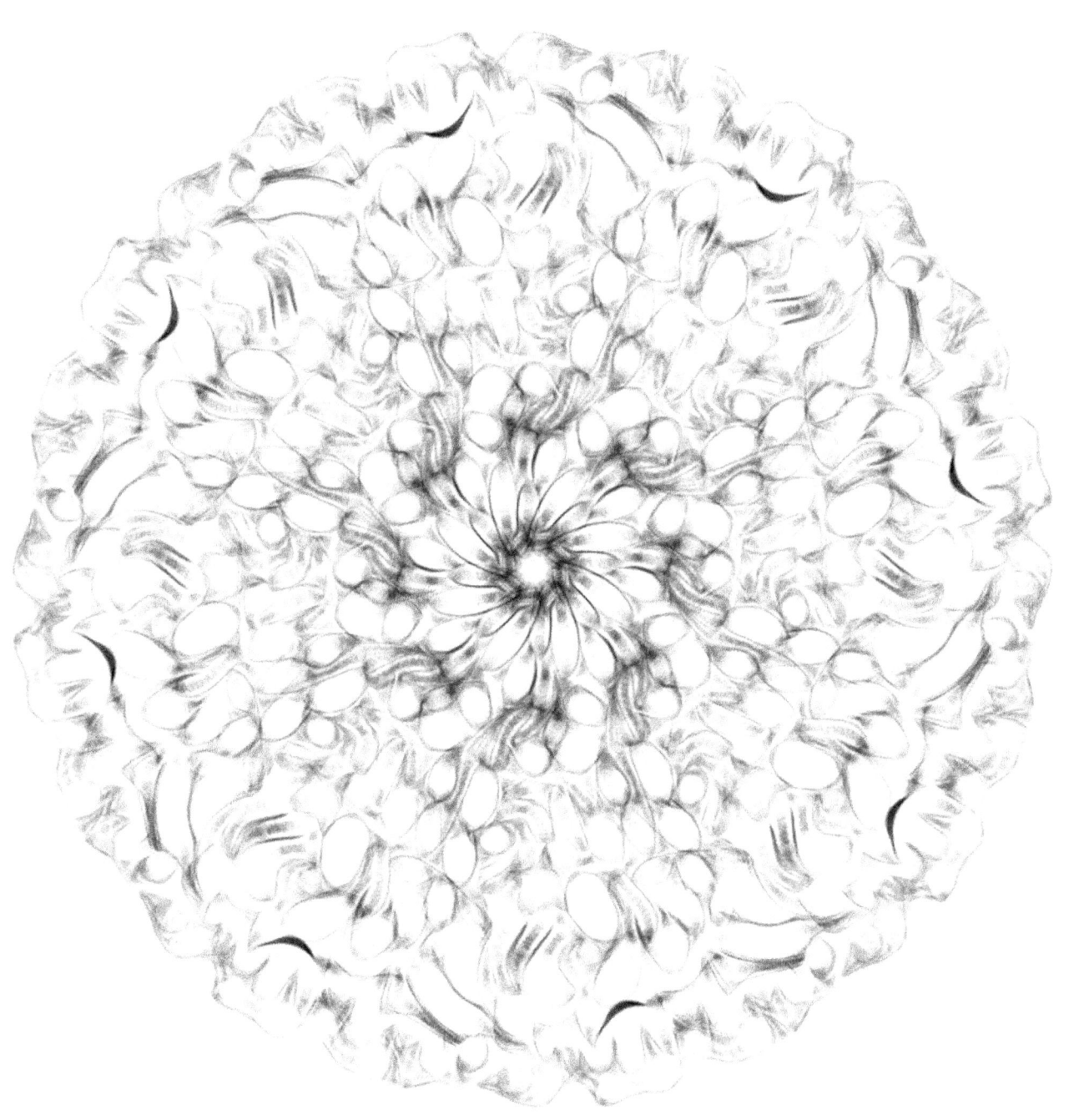

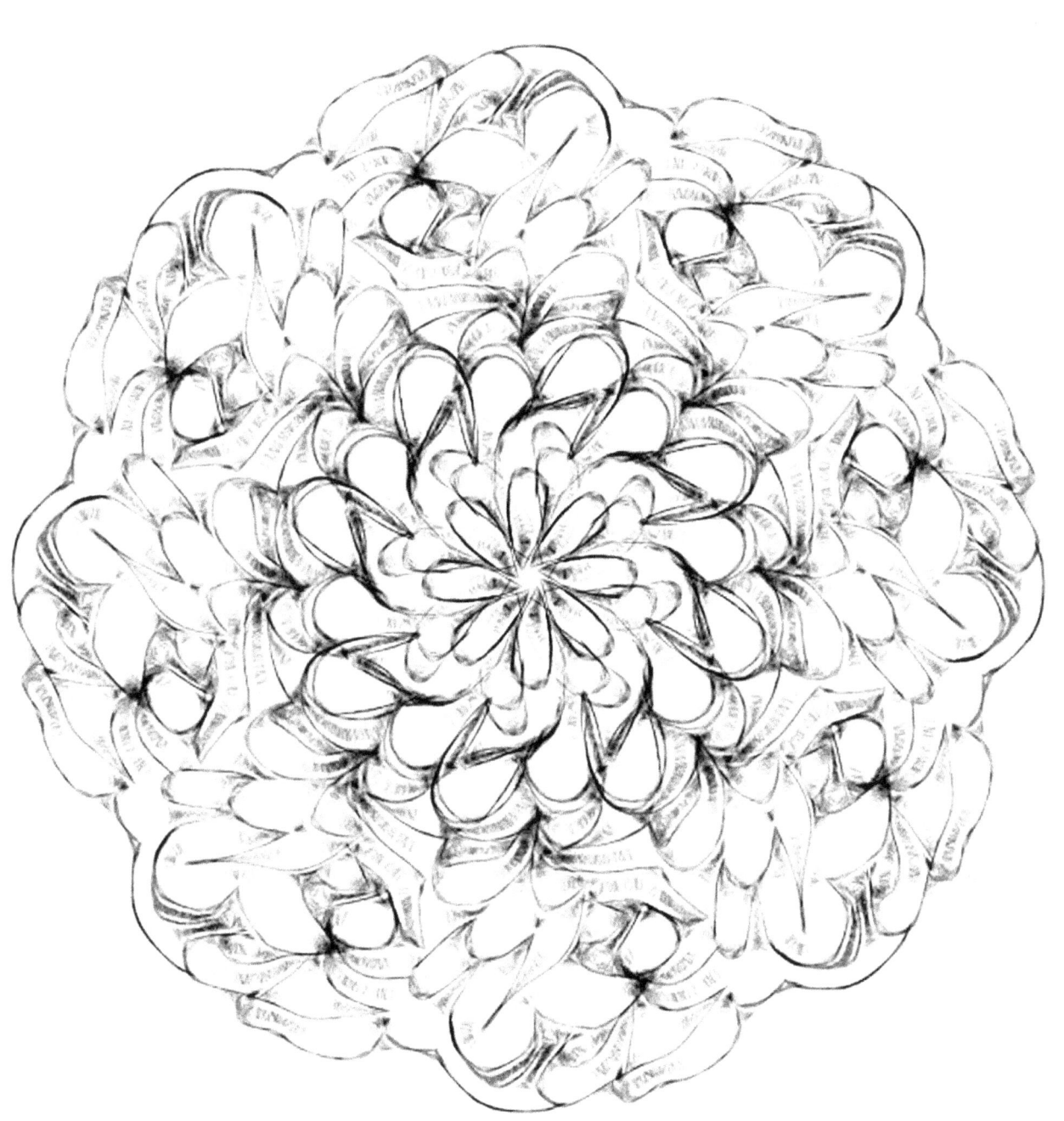

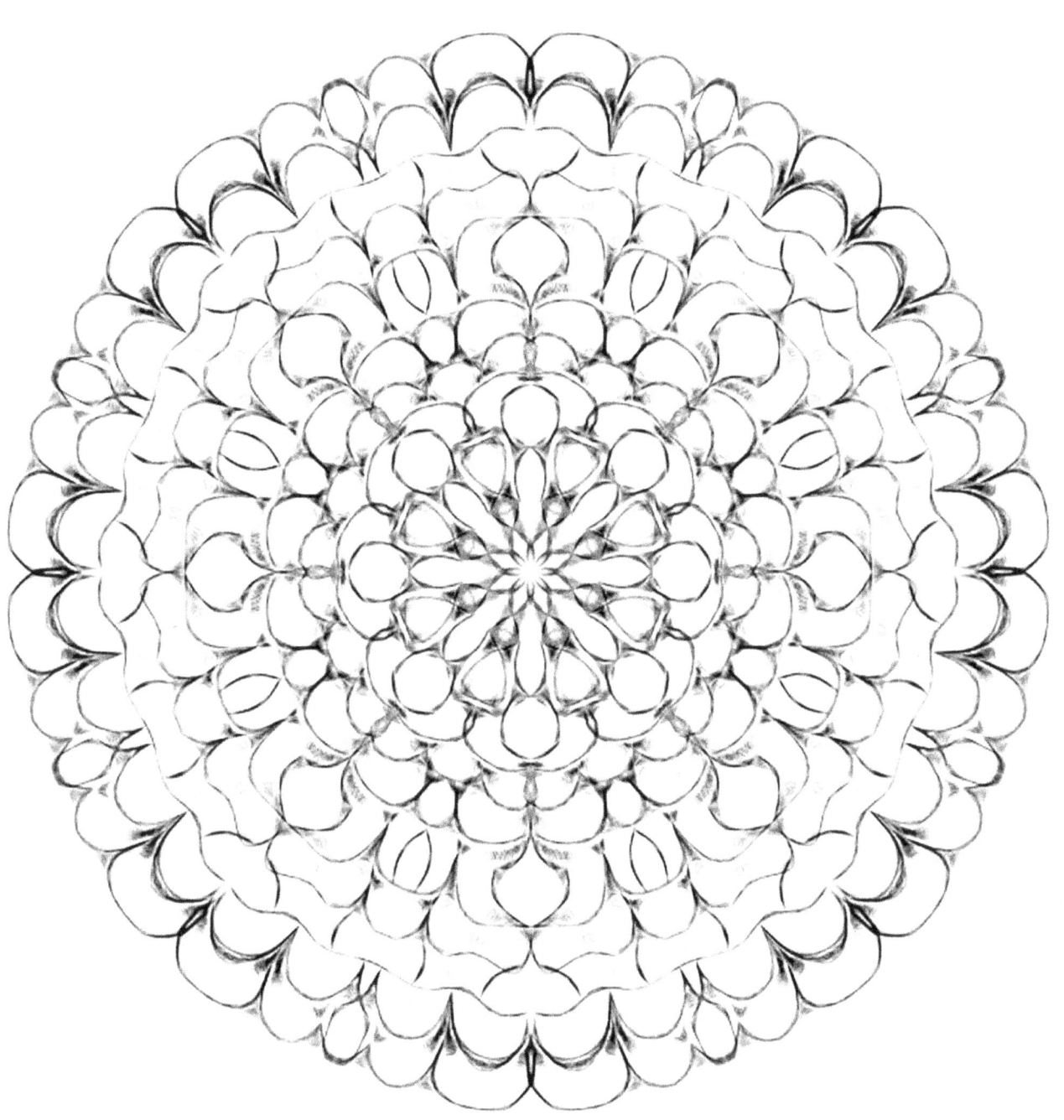

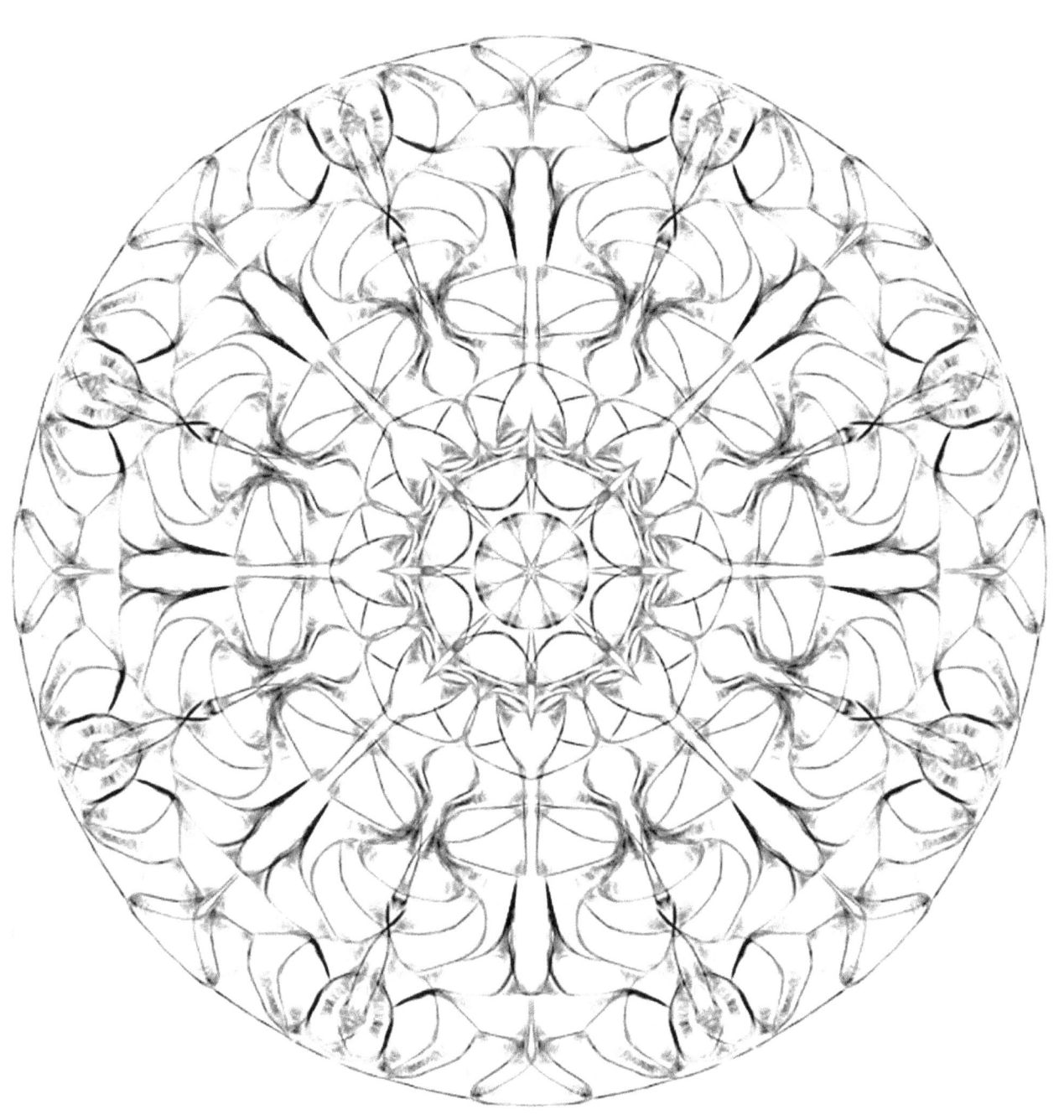

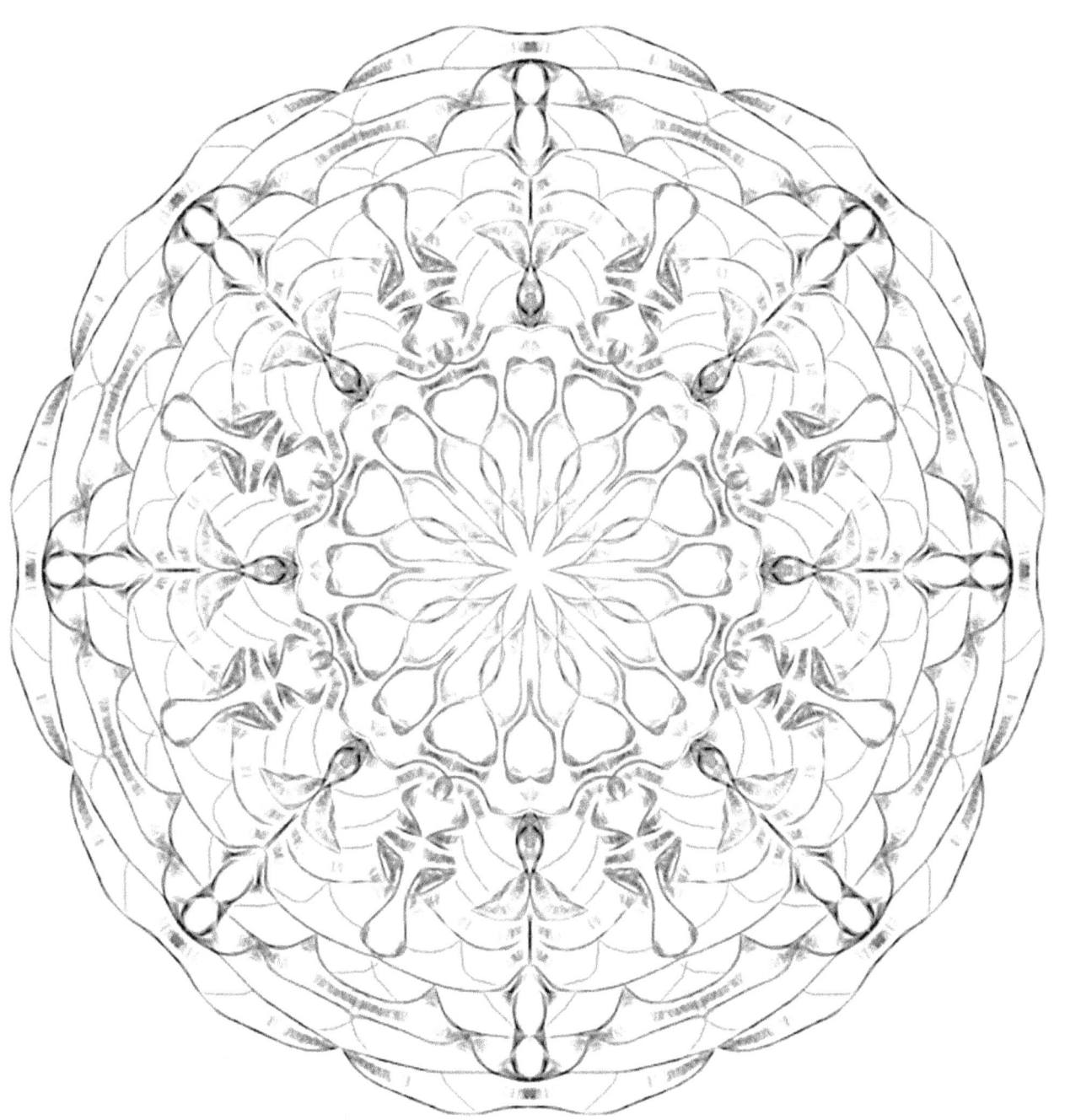

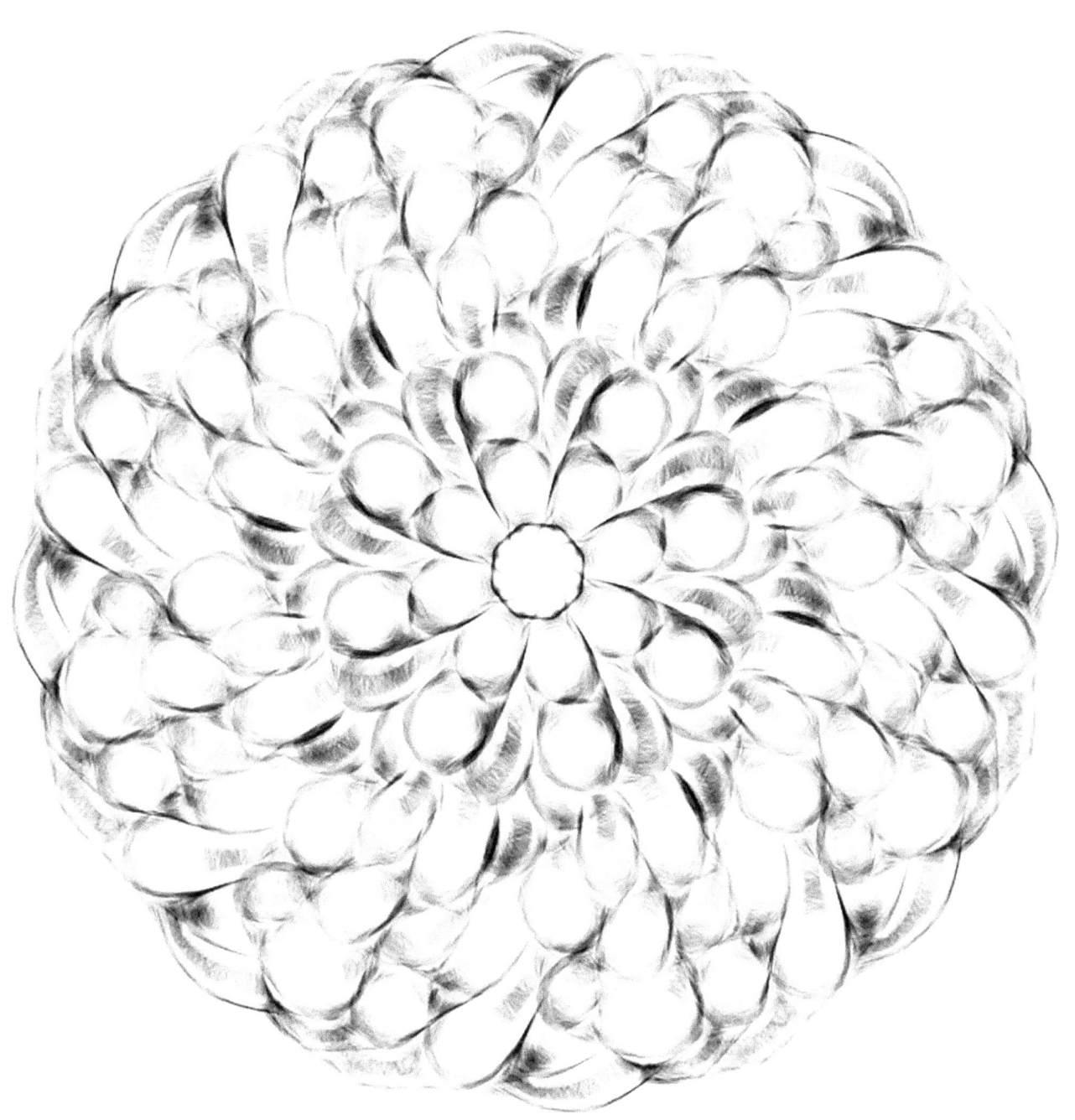

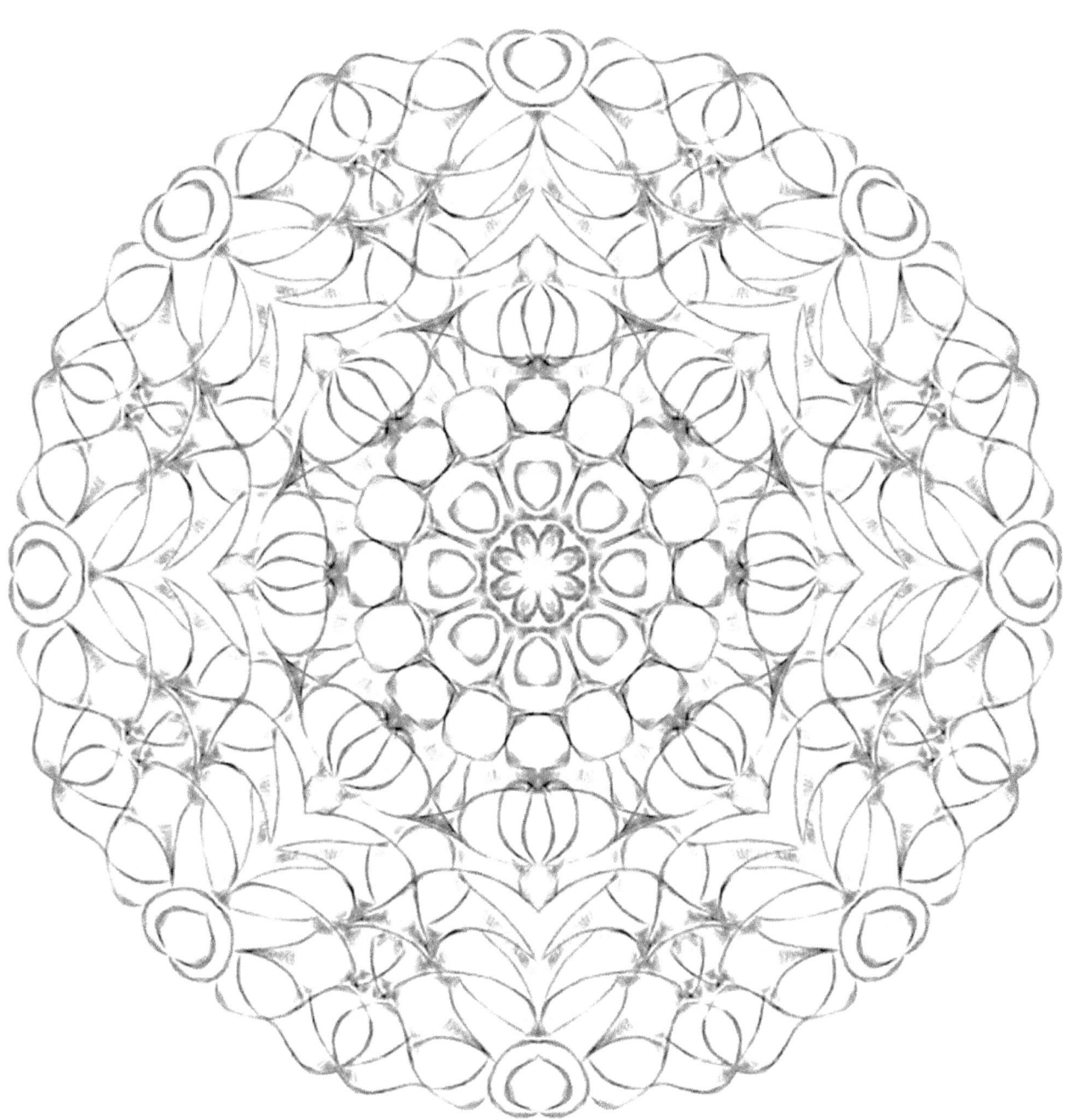

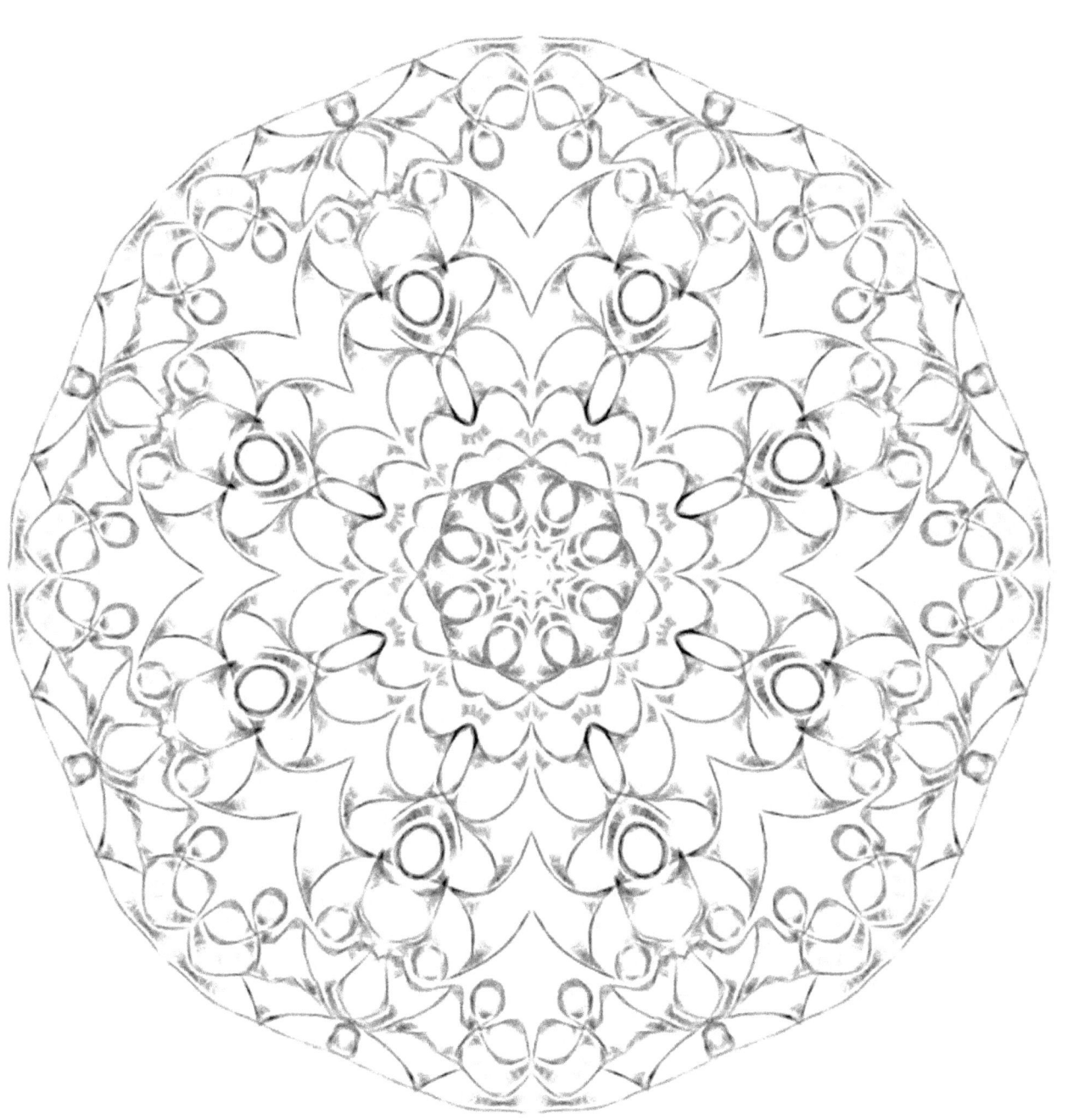

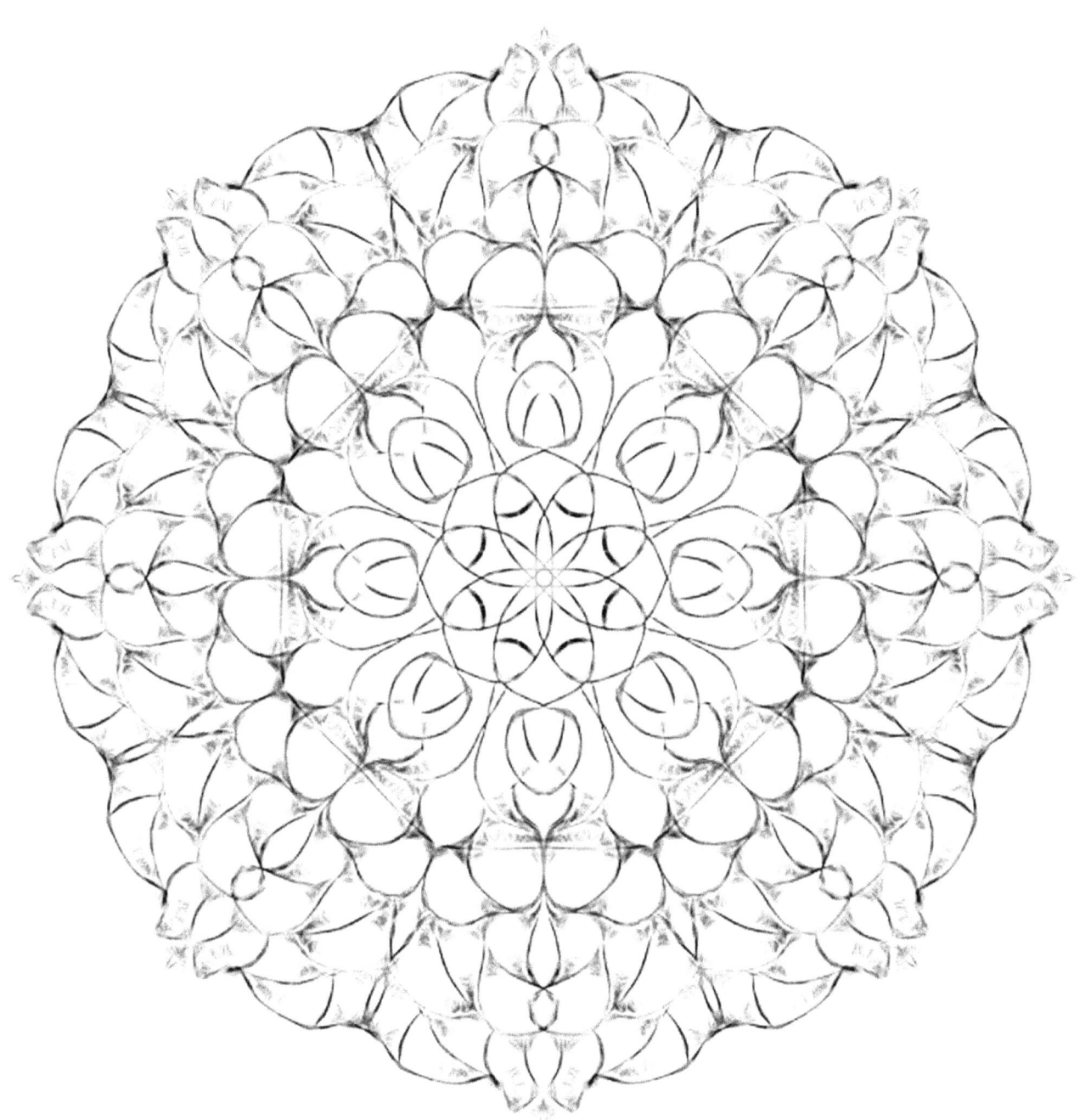

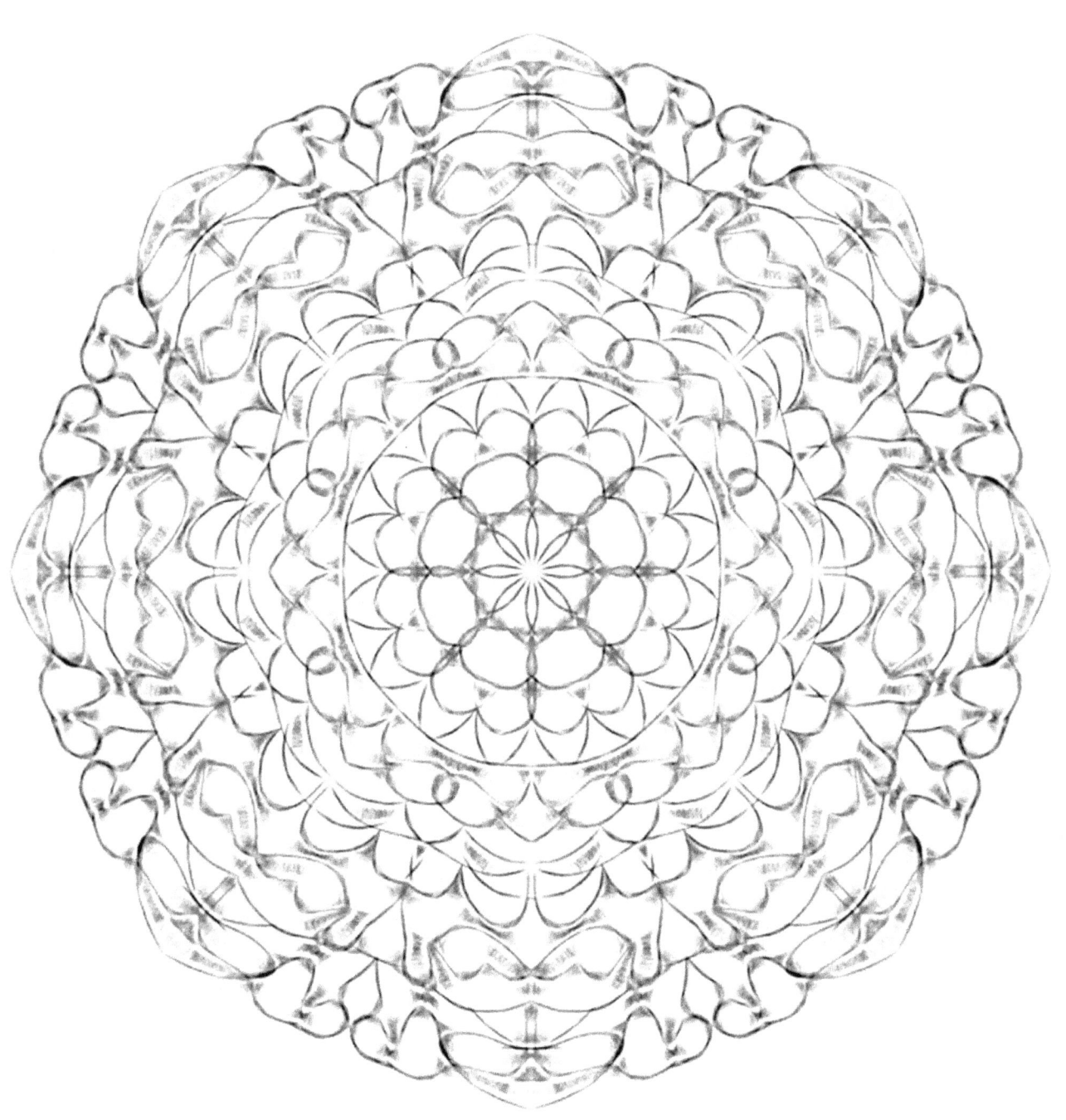

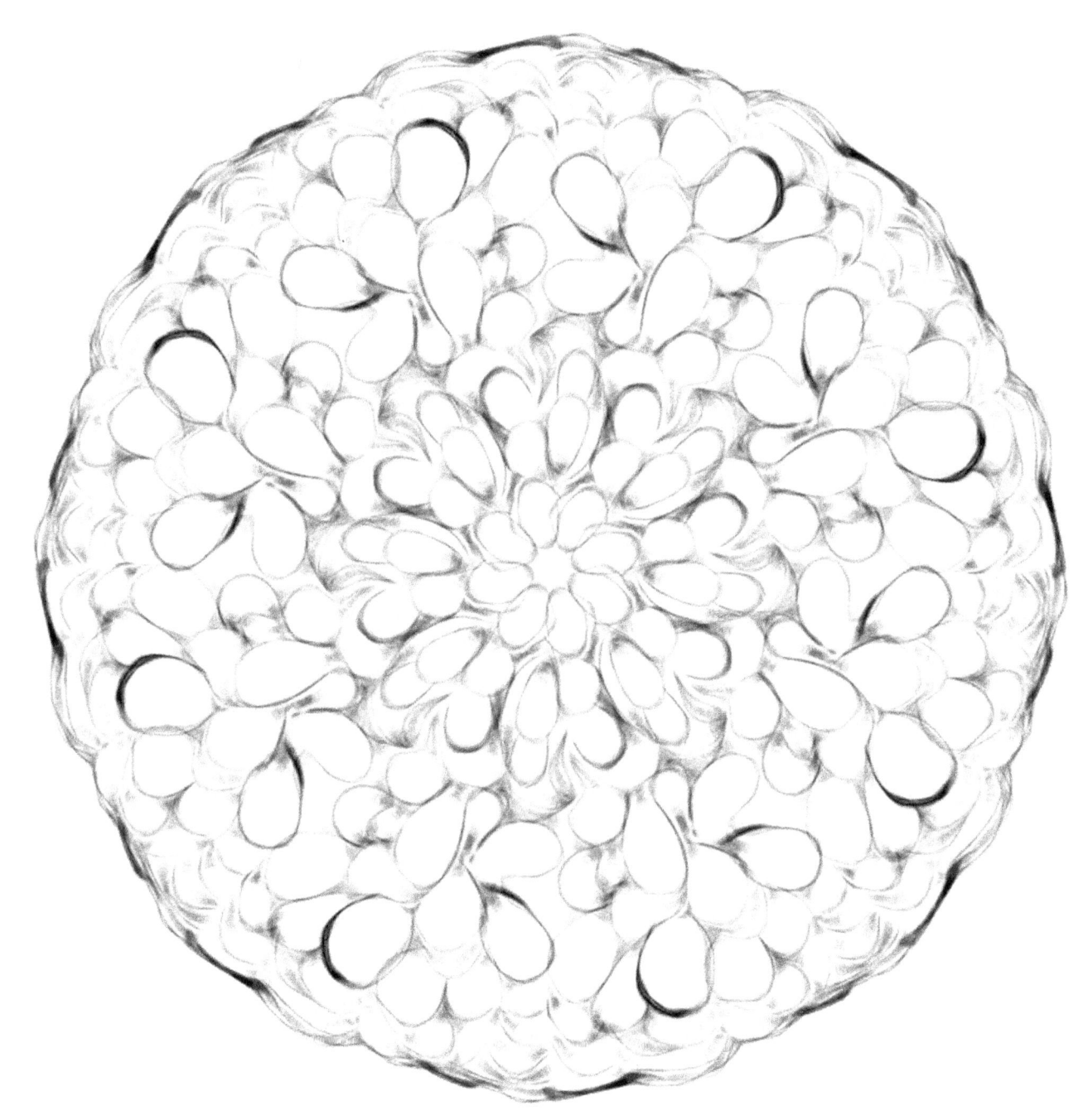

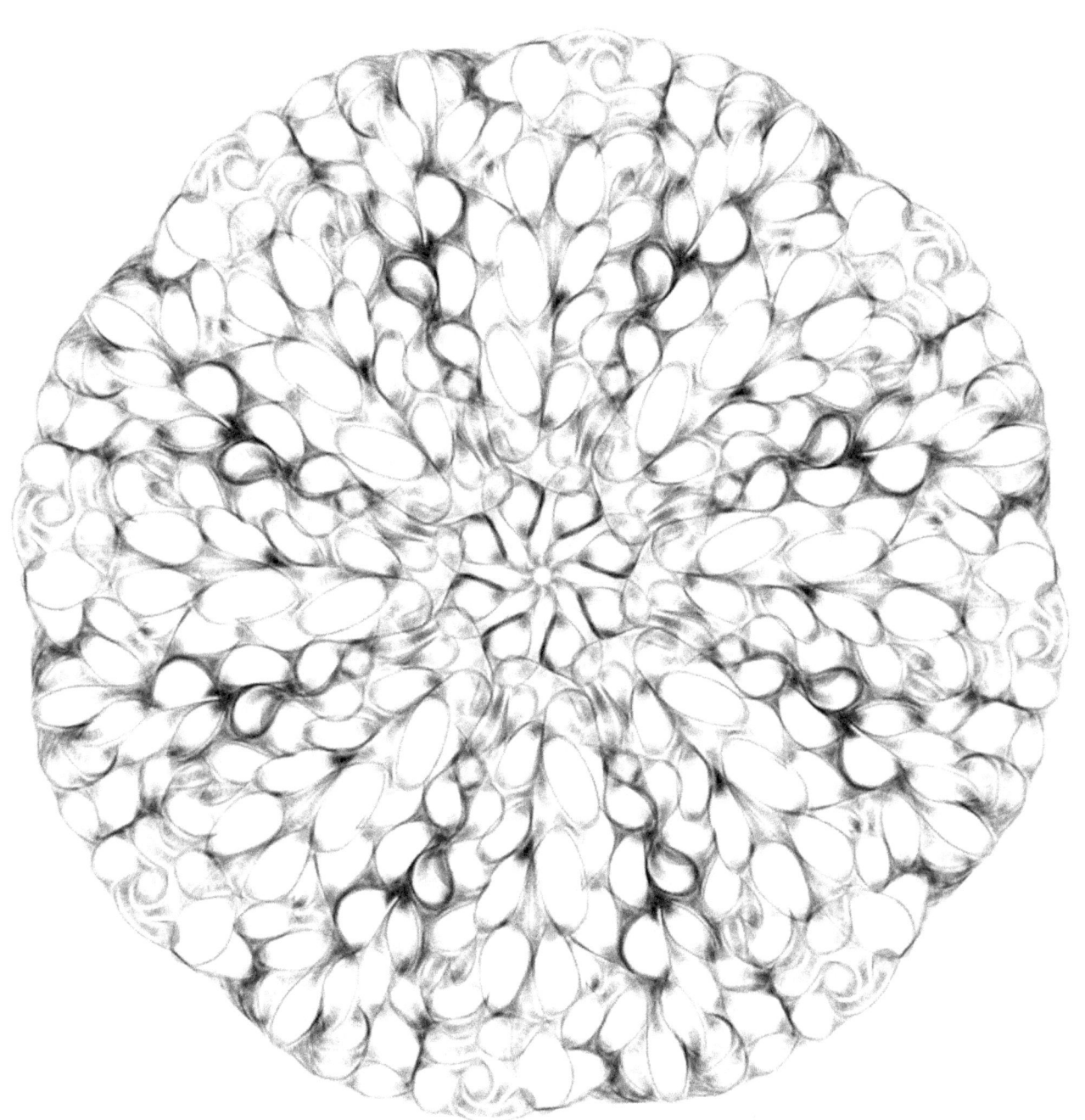

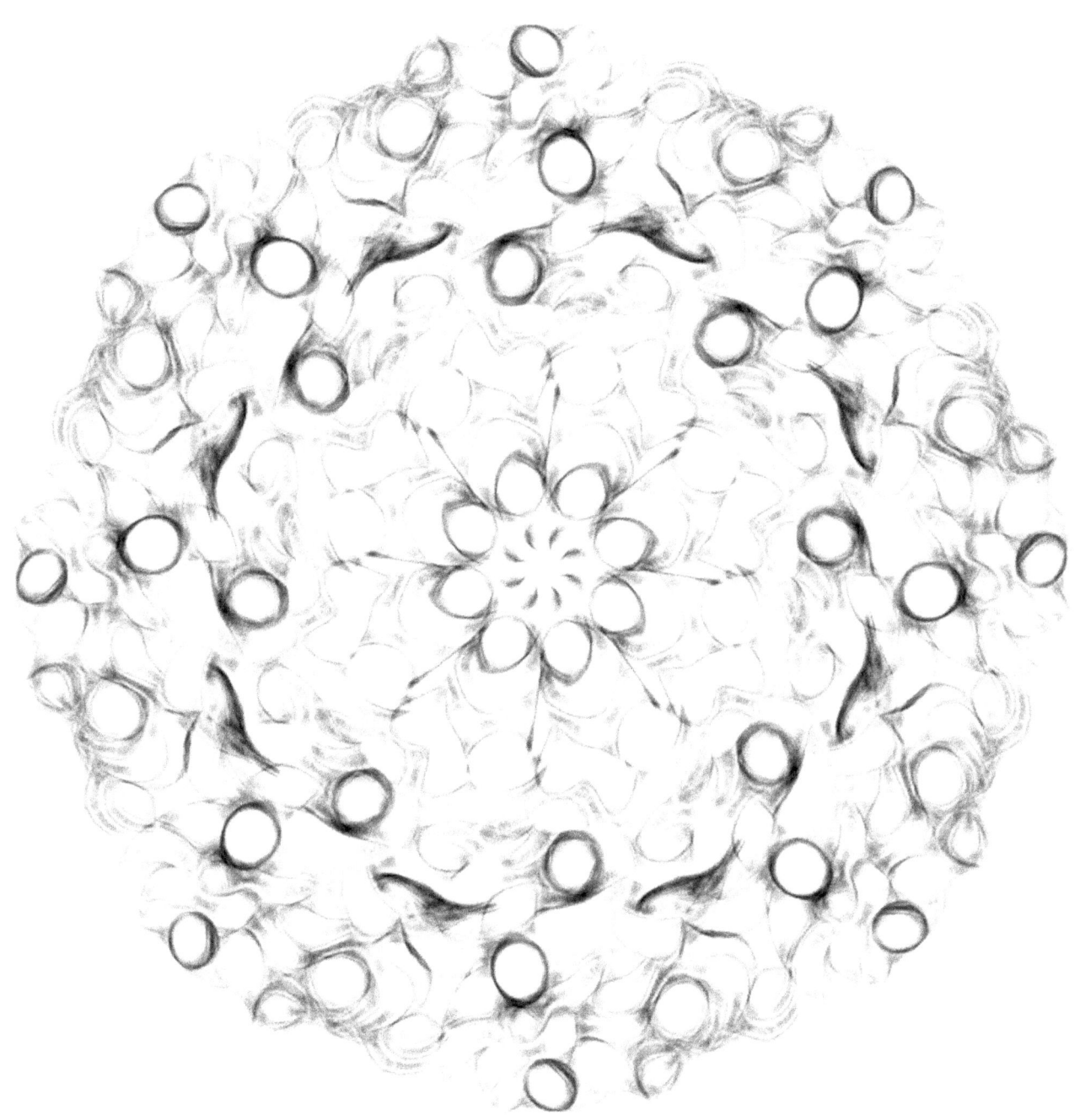

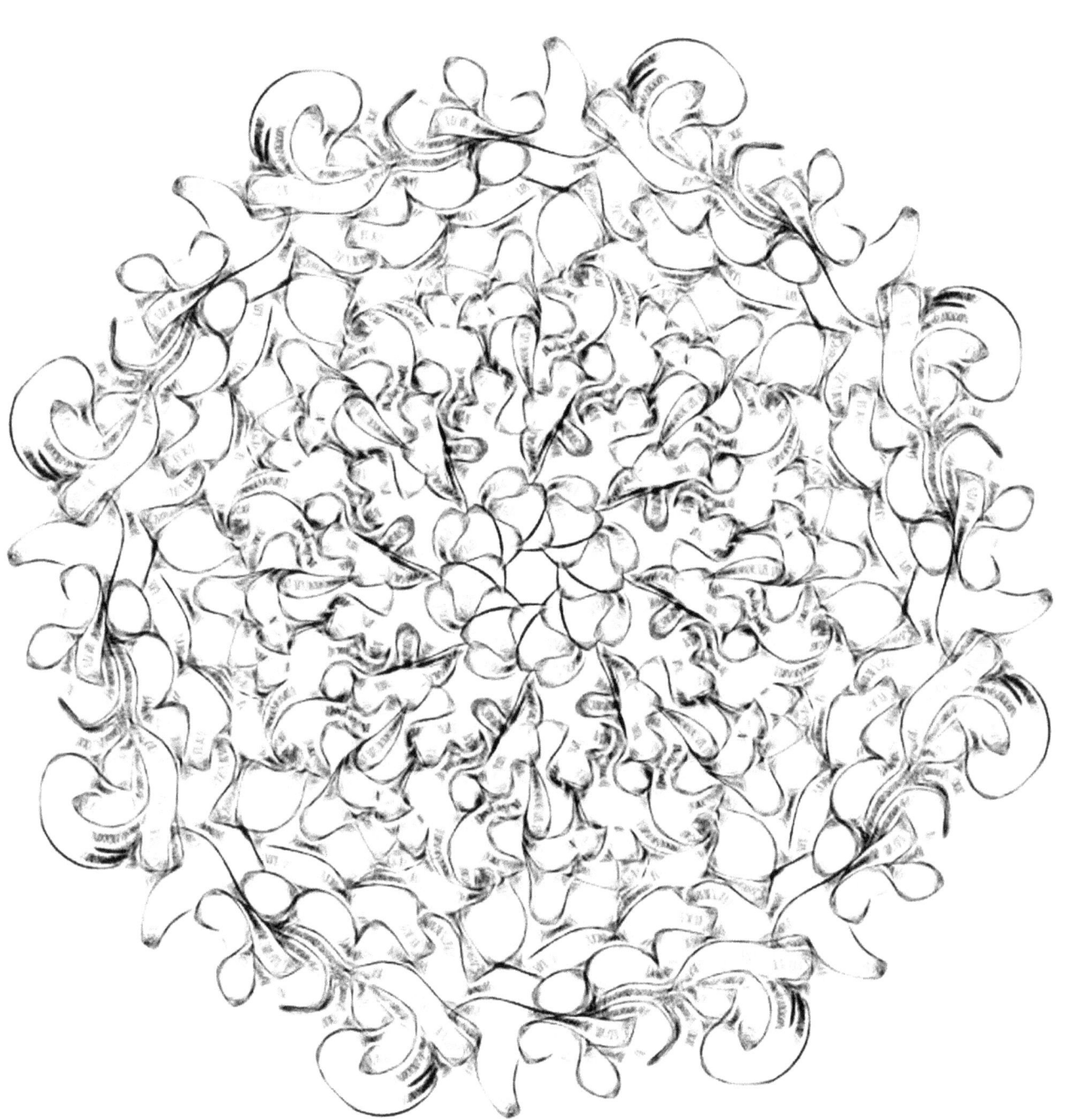

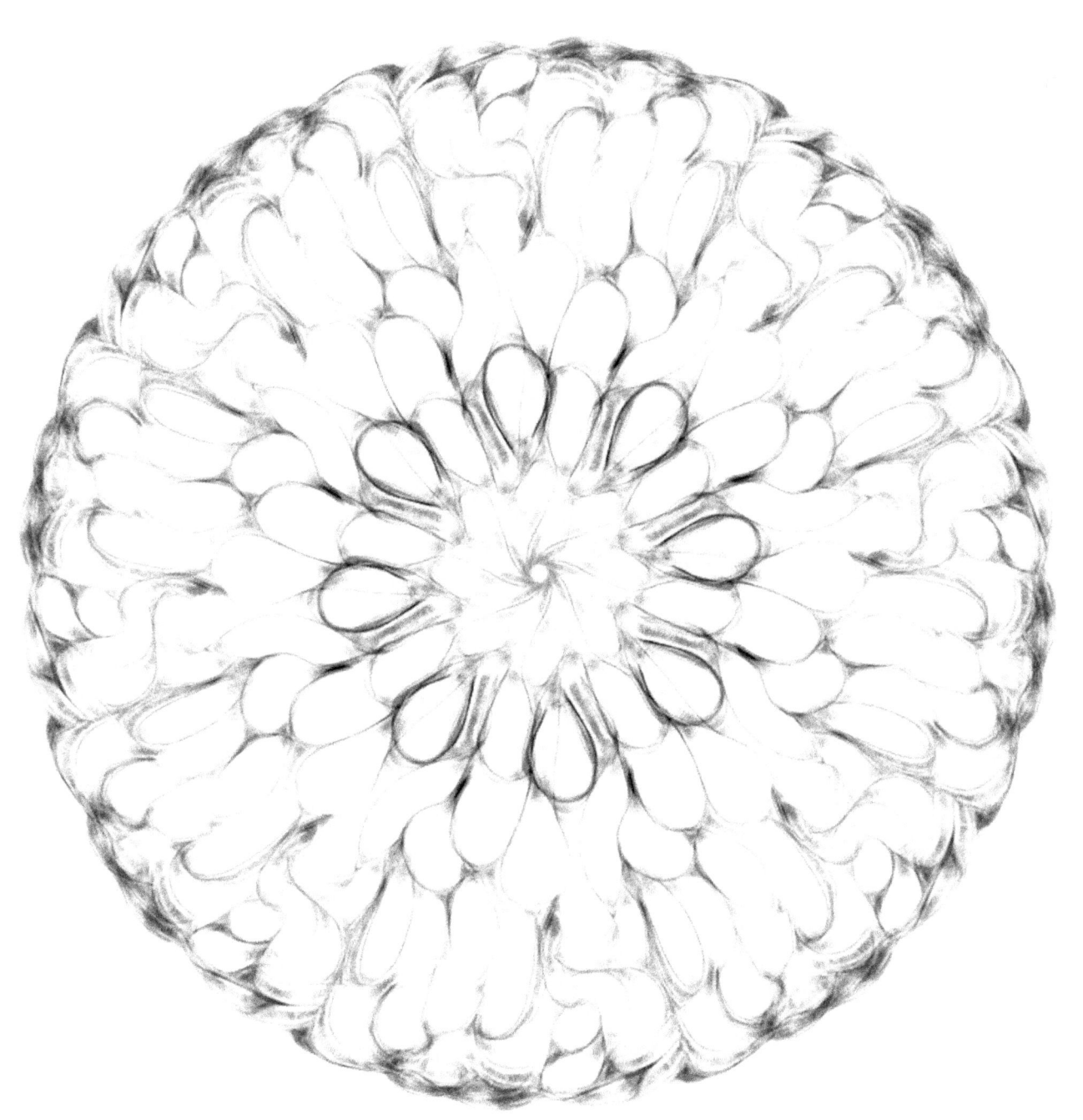

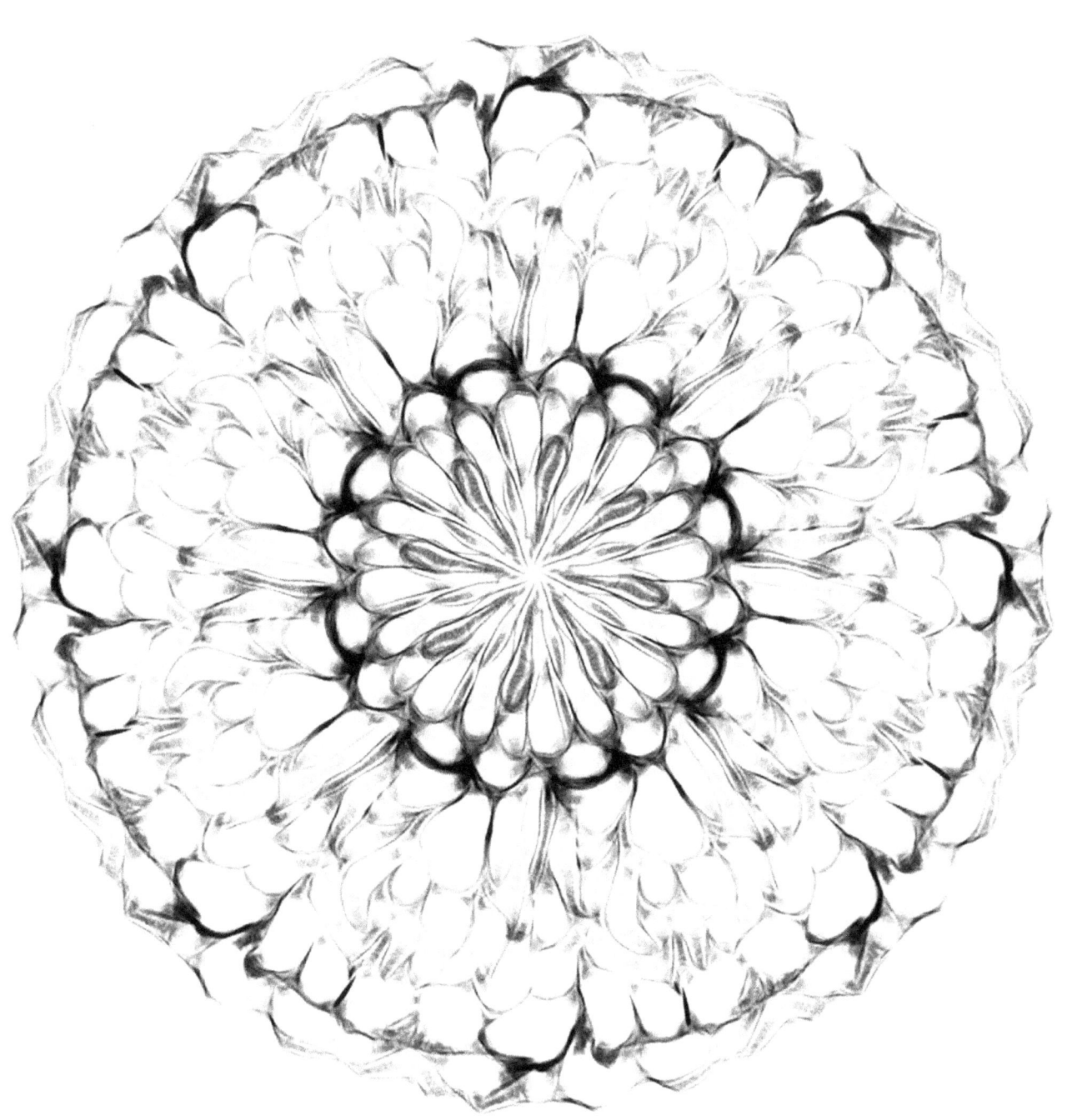

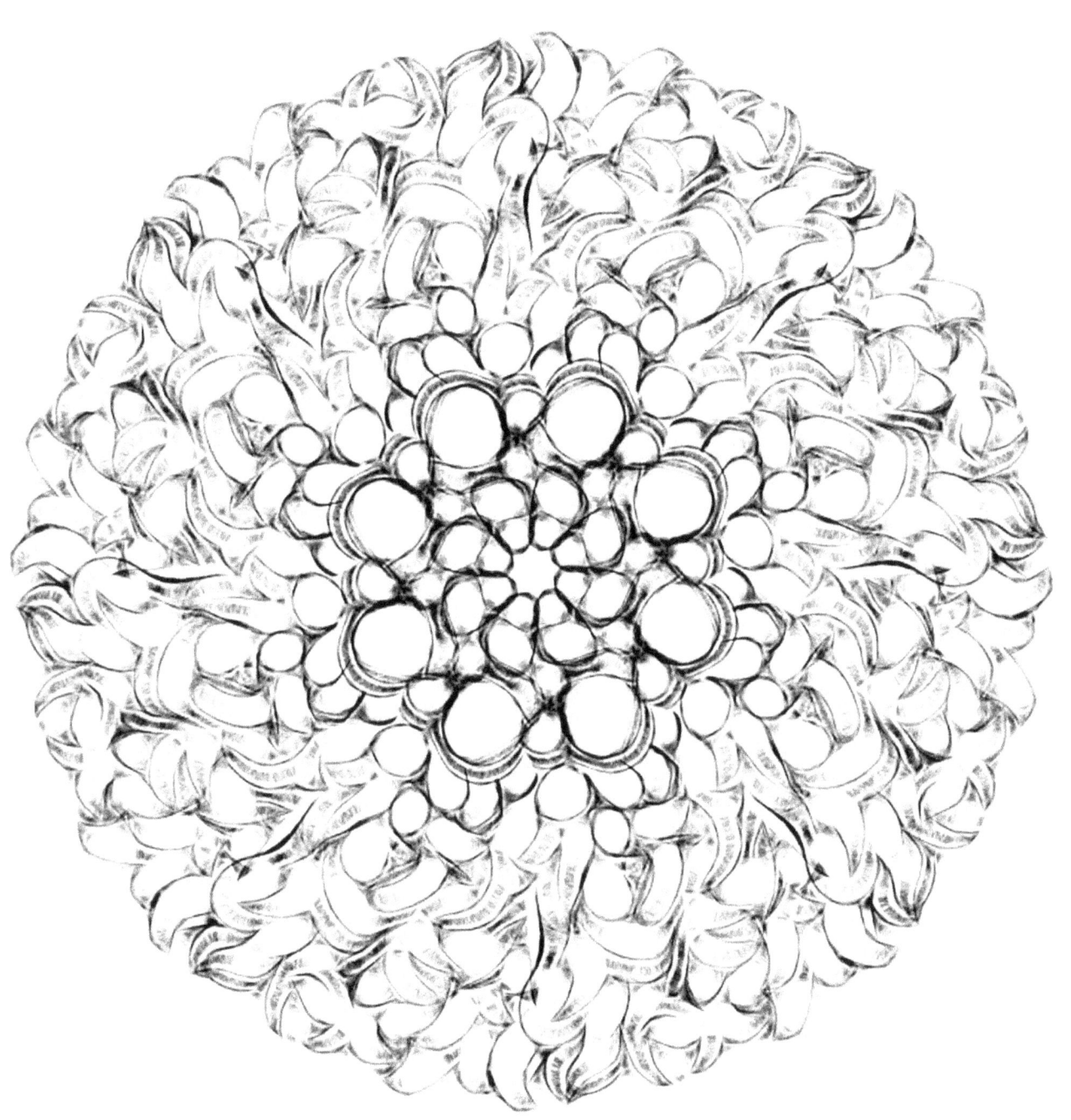

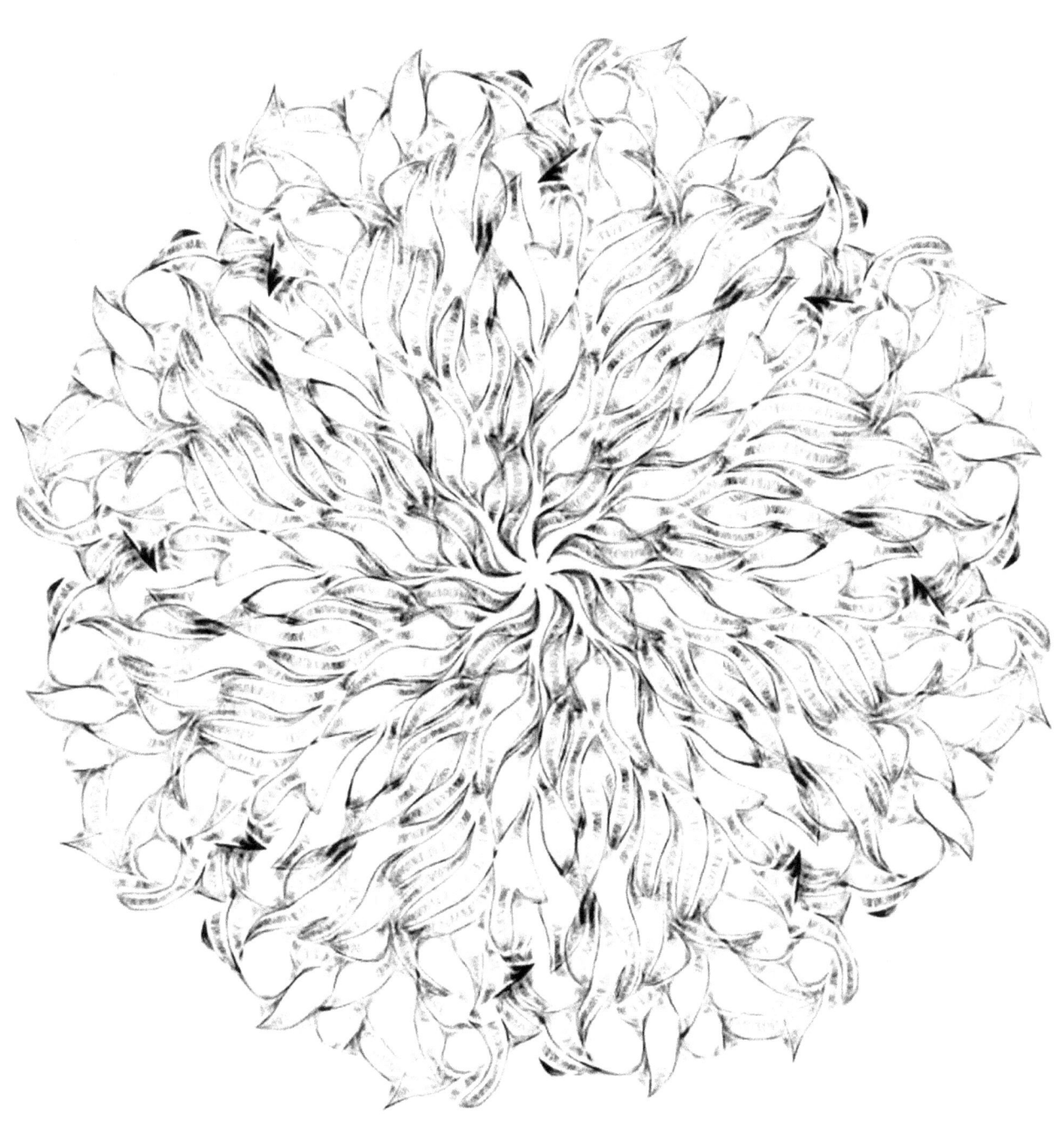

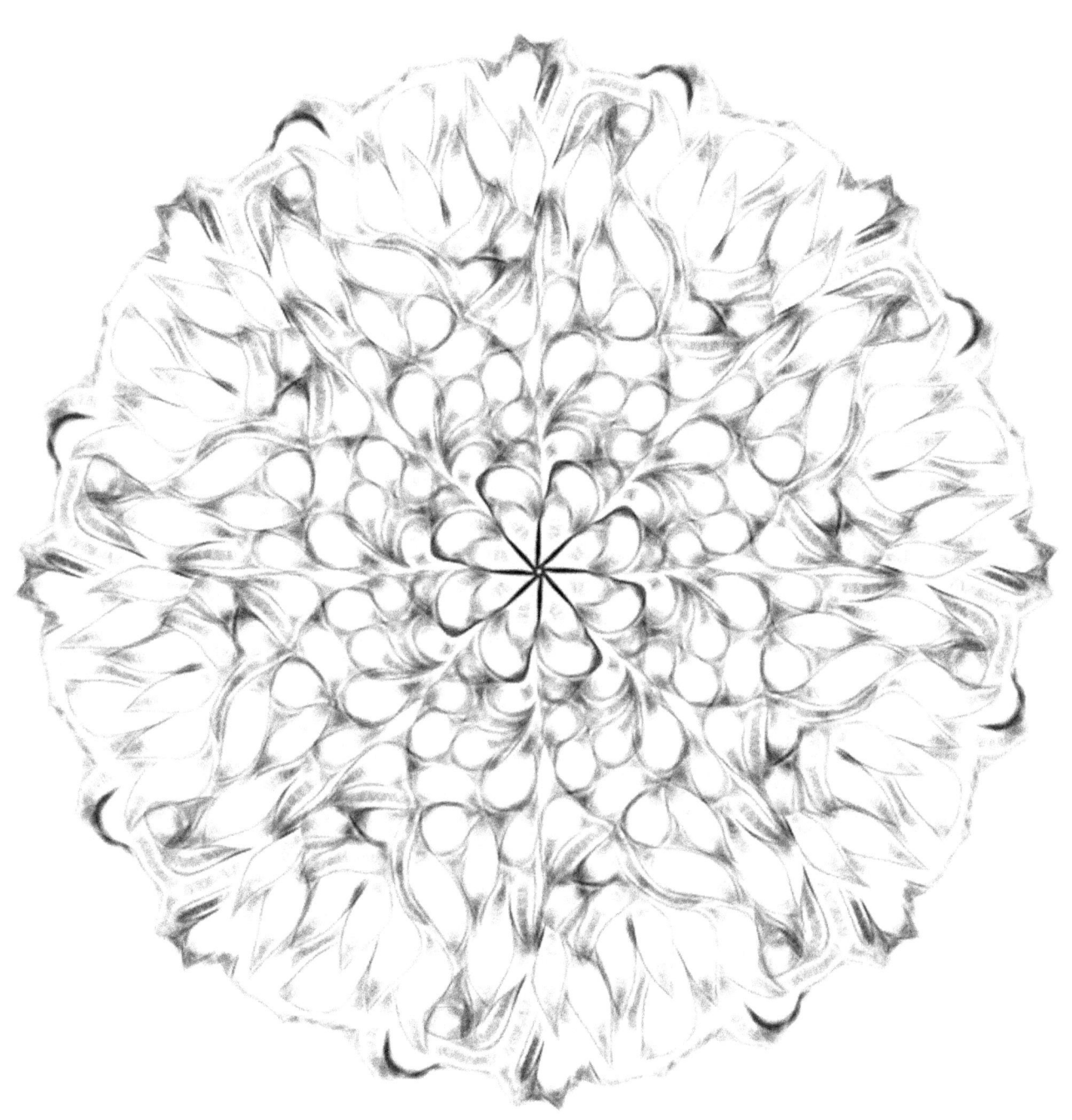

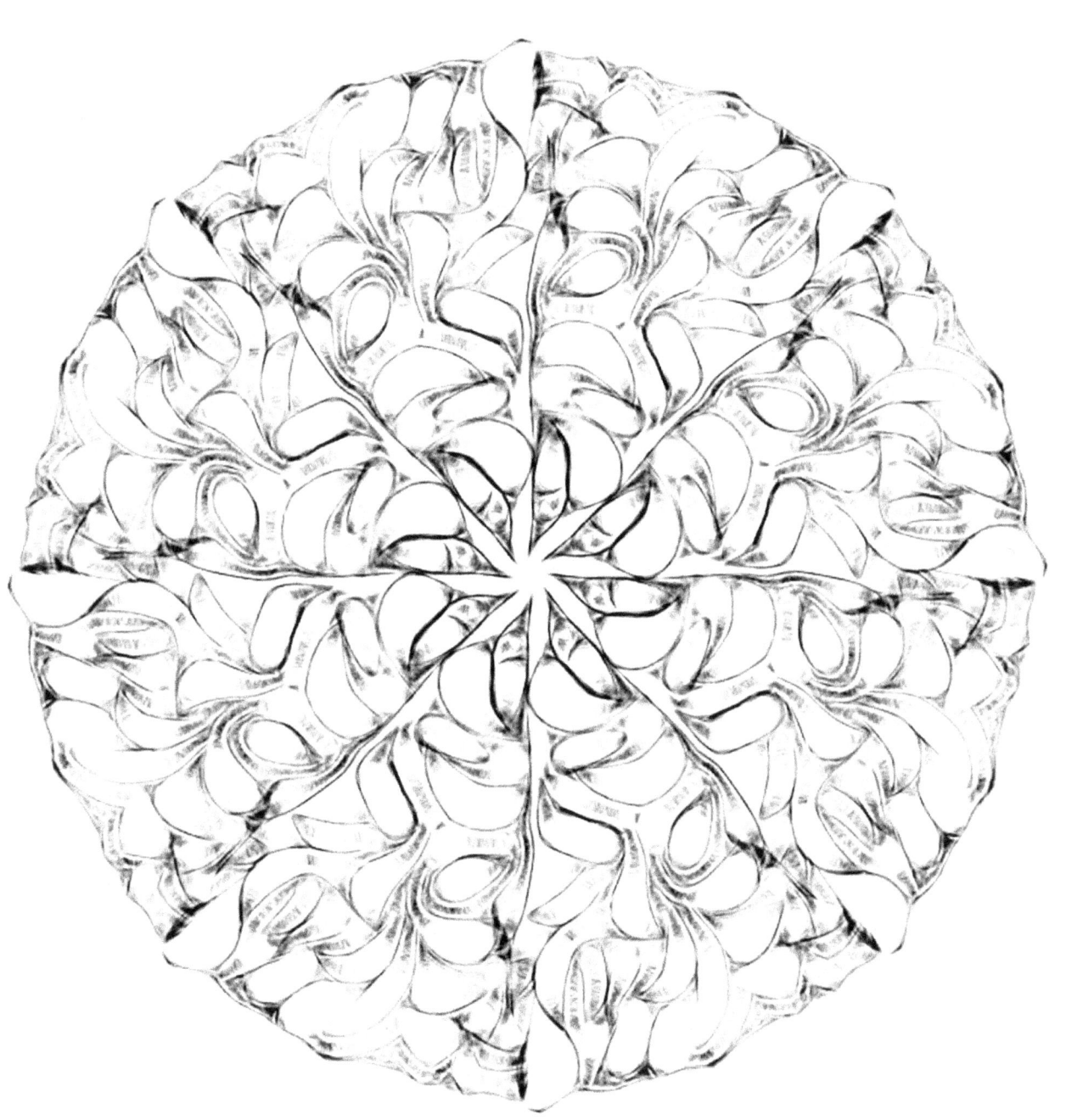

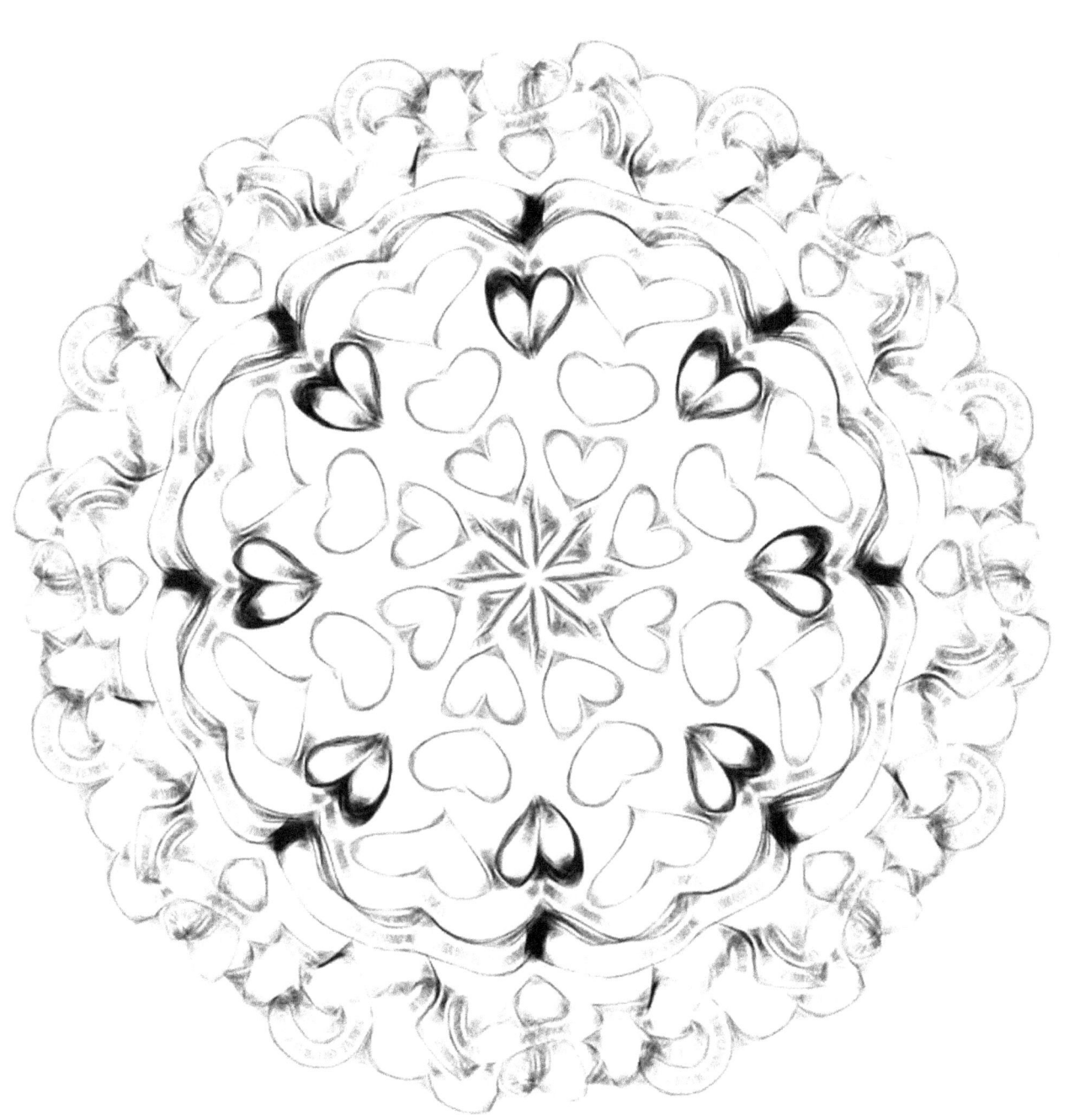

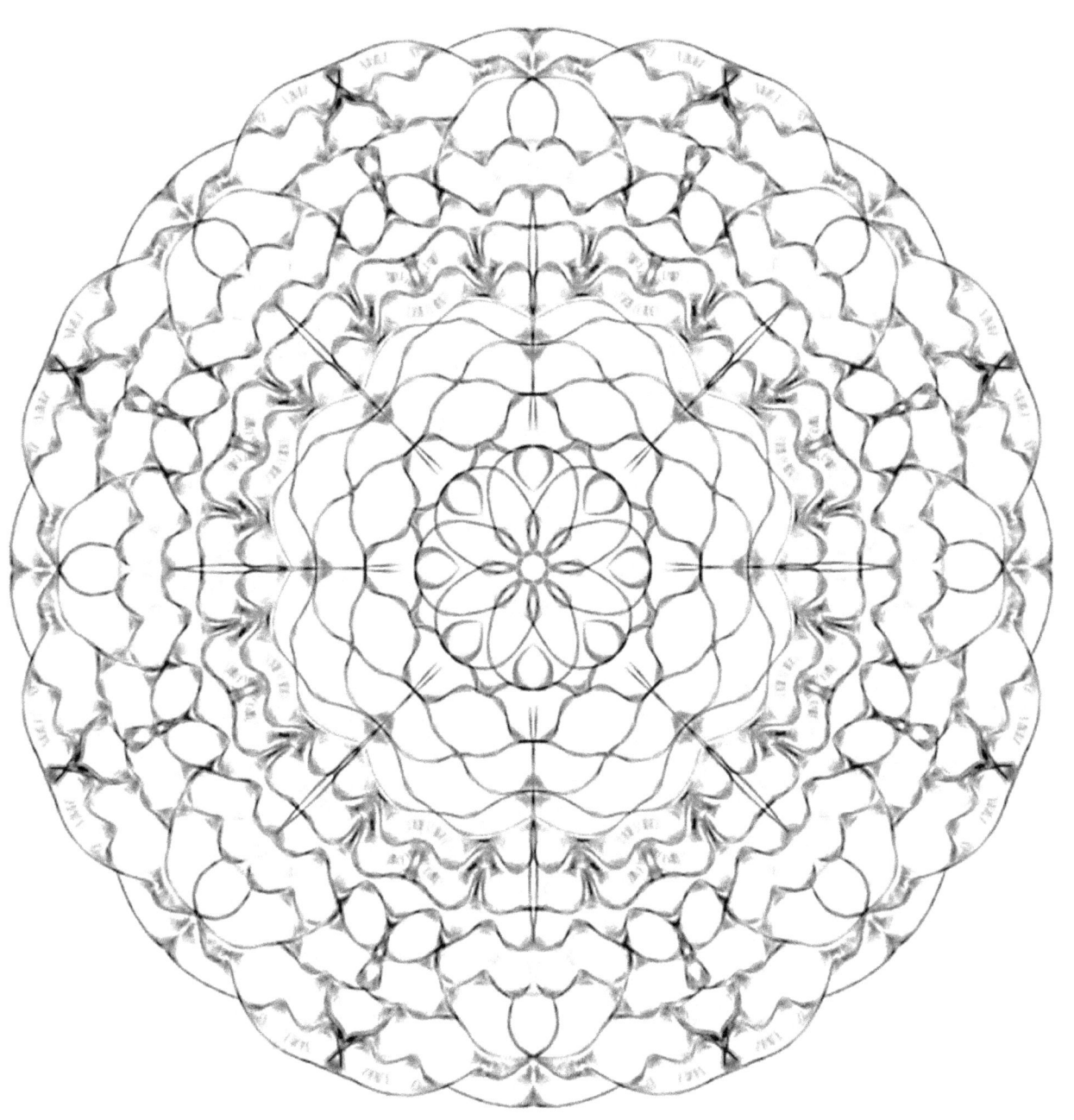

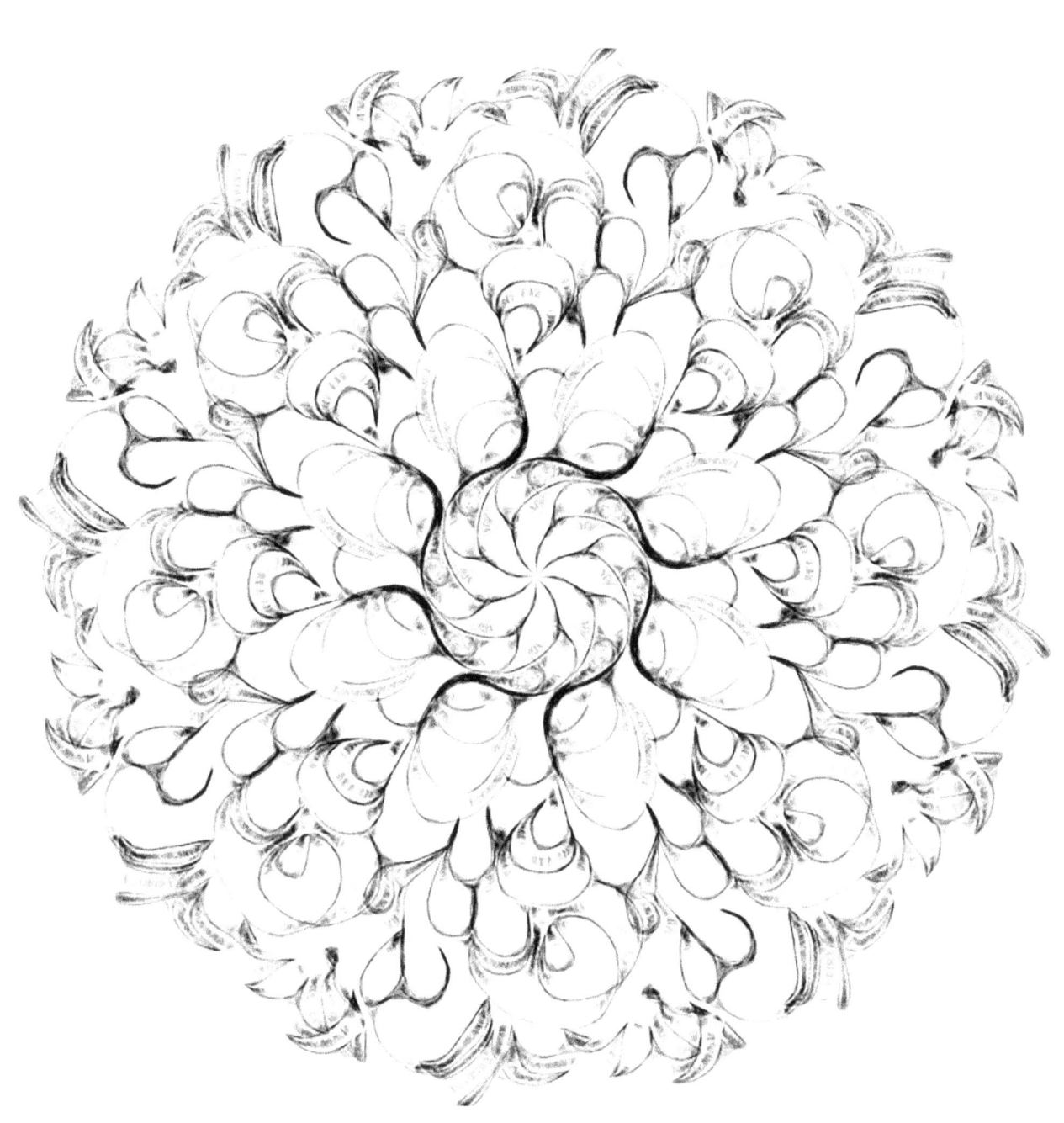

www.ingramcontent.com/pod-product-compliance
Lightning Source LLC
Chambersburg PA
CBHW082303200526
45168CB00017B/2764